Living with a
Dachshund

Edited by Sheila Shuker

RINGPRESS

THE QUESTION OF GENDER
**The 'he' pronoun is used throughout this book in favour of the rather impersonal 'it',
but no gender bias is intended at all.**

ACKNOWLEDGEMENTS

Elizabeth Heeson (for some photos and contribution to Chapter One); Brenda and Trevor Humphrey, and Nick Valentine (for photos and contribution to the working Teckel, Chapter Six); Mrs Hosegood; Mrs Goad; Mrs Punter; Val Beynon (training/troubleshooting).

The publisher would also like to thank the following for help with photography:
Sheila Shuker (Yewllitt), Gladys Mead (Minimead), Nina Dible (Liebling), Carol Worswick (Dolyharp), Jason Hunt (Carpaccio) and Yvonne Angear (Ridgegrove).

Published by Ringpress Books Ltd,
PO Box 8, Lydney,
Gloucestershire GL15 4YN

Series Director: Claire Horton-Bussey

Designed by Rob Benson.

First Published 2002
© 2002 RINGPRESS BOOKS

ALL RIGHTS RESERVED

ISBN 1 86054 206 9

Printed and bound in Singapore
0 9 8 7 6 5 4 3 2 1

CONTENTS

CHAPTER ONE

INTRODUCING THE DACHSHUND

With his super-long body, short legs, and expressive face, the Dachshund is like no other breed of dog. He is one of the smaller hounds, but what he lacks in size he makes up for in courage, determination and cunning.

In the UK, the Kennel Club Standard describes the Dachshund – or Teckel, as he is also known – as "bold to the point of foolhardiness", a sentiment shared by US enthusiasts.

The American Kennel Club says the breed is "clever, lively and courageous to the point of rashness".

This daring, adventurous side of the Dachshund's character comes to the fore the moment he gets a sniff of the great outdoors, when he reverts to his working past.

Indoors, however, when the Dachshund is off-duty, he can be a most affectionate pet – cuddly, playful, full of fun.

WORKING HERITAGE

Small, short-legged hounds have existed for centuries and are depicted on Egyptian tombs, and in early clay, stone, wood and china models, found in South America, China, France and Greece. Although short-legged, the similarity with the early dogs depicted ends there – most had erect ears, long, pointed muzzles, and some are even said to resemble pigs!

Skeletons not dissimilar to that of the Dachshund have also been found. Bronze Age canine skeletons have been found in Silesia (northern Czech Republic), and in Roman ruins in Germany.

These dogs could have been the early relatives of the modern-day Dachshund, and were all used to hunt in their various countries.

ST. HUBERT'S LEGACY

It is widely accepted that the Dachshund descends from the St. Hubert Hound, a hunting breed that was developed by the St. Hubert monks in Ardennes, Belgium. St. Hubert, who lived from 656 to 727 AD, was considered fairly outrageous in his day, rejecting worship on holy days in favour of hunting with his hounds.

One Good Friday, he refused to attend church, and set off for a nearby forest. He was about to shoot a magnificent white stag with his bow and arrow, when a cross appeared between the animal's antlers. Hubert immediately repented, and attended church straight away. He confessed his sins, and thereafter led an exemplary life, devoting himself to the church. Hunting remained a passion, however, and the monastery, founded in his name, continued to keep and breed hunting hounds long after St. Hubert died.

Sadly, the St. Hubert Hound is now extinct, but there is considerable documentation about the breed. The dog was low to the ground, with a long body, and excellent scenting ability. Many hounds are believed to have descended from the St. Hubert Hound, including the Beagle, the Basset Hound, and the Dachshund.

GERMAN DEVELOPMENT

In 1477, Maximilian I, the Holy Roman Emperor (and heir to the Hapsburg throne), travelled from Vienna to Burgundy to marry Marie, the Duke of Burgundy's daughter. The Duke was a wealthy, powerful man, with extensive hunting land – it was so extensive that he kept 4,000 hounds! Maximilian and his accompanying noblemen were deeply impressed by these hounds and they took several with them back to Austria.

Early German Dachshunds.

It is possible that these hounds – short-legged descendants of the St. Hubert Hound – were then bred with native German breeds, such as the Dachskrieger, the Huhnerhund, and the Wachtelhund. The actual facts remain hidden in time.

FORESTERS' FRIEND

It is the German foresters and huntsmen we should thank for the creation of the Dachshund. In the early 17th and 18th centuries, there were enormous forests in Germany, alive with game of every sort, not only rabbits, deer, fox, and badger, but also wild boar.

The foresters wanted a dog capable not only of tracking and scenting out game, but who was also low enough to hunt below ground. The hound needed a sufficiently bold temperament to hold his prey at bay, and he then had to bark long and loud enough for the hunter to locate him and dig down to the prey. The work required a hardy dog who could follow and

A German forester with his dog after a day's work.

track the larger prey through thick undergrowth and rocky terrain; then, when the prey was found (perhaps wounded or dead), the dog was expected to stand guard over it and Totverbel (give tongue) until the huntsman arrived.

BADGER DOGS

In the early days, the first dogs used for this type of work were the Dachsbracke, hunting hounds still being used today. Dachs means badger and Bracke comes from the verb Brecken, to break, meaning that the hound had to break through thick undergrowth.

The foresters selected the smallest, lowest specimens of Dachsbracke, which generally have quite long legs, and carefully bred these dogs to low-legged breeds, such as the Basset Hound and the Beagle. In later years, the most successful outcross was to the Schweisshund, the small short-legged German Bloodhound. It is from this dog that the Dachshund has inherited his wonderful scenting ability.

THE DACHSHUND EMERGES

These early dogs were recorded under many delightful names – 'Lockhundlein' (Little Burrow Dog), 'Dachschlieffer' (Badger Burrower), and 'Erdhundle' (Little Earth Dog).

The evidence of the mixed blood of these early Dachshunds is found in contemporary descriptions, which list many different coat colours (white, black, yellow, red, dappled and brindle). Some were called straight-legged or crooked-legged, and some sported rough hair.

These early Dachshunds were probably quite fierce, as they had been bred to do dangerous work, and, as late as 1812, Dr Walther, one of the early enthusiasts, wrote: "They are snappy, often pugnacious, brave but quarrelsome; tenacious of life, they tend to engage with any dog, be he ever so big."

The foresters did not keep large numbers of hounds, and so any that did not make the grade (such as the gentler, less fierce dogs) would be given as pets to the landowner's family. This was undoubtedly the beginning of the great rise in popularity of the breed – the Dachshund proved that he was not only a worker in the forests, but also a loving and faithful companion in the home.

RISE OF THE BREED

The Dachshund gained entry to the German Stud Book (which records the breeding details of pedigree dogs), and by 1840 there were 54 Dachshunds registered (in Volume I).

Wilhelm von Daacke has earned a place in Dachshund history as one of the most

The Germans were anxious that the Dachshund or Teckel should always be bred as a hunting dog.

influential of the early breeders. He was based in Osterode in the Harz Mountains, in central Germany, and specialised in breeding small reds, specifically for the hunt. Von Daacke started to breed in 1868, taking for his motto 'Der Teckel ist als Jagshund zu züchten' – 'the Teckel should always be bred as a hunting dog'.

It was von Daacke who used the German Bloodhound in his breeding programme, and he stated that the ideal size should be about 17 lbs (7.72 kgs) for a male dog, and a female should weigh a pound (0.45 kg) less, considerably smaller than the standard-sized varieties seen today (see page 102). In fact, the Germans have maintained their love of the very small Dachshund and have an extra, third, size, not seen in the United States or Britain – the

Kaninchenteckel (rabbit Dachshund), no larger than 6 $1/2$ lbs (3 kgs), which was used specifically for rabbit-hunting.

Other famous names of this period were Major Emil Ilgner and Dr Fritz Engelmann. Both were primarily interested in the Dachshund as a hunting dog, and Major Ilgner was the first president of the Teckel Klub, founded in 1888.

Smooth-haired

Dachshunds were generally smooth-coated in the early days of the breed, but it wasn't long before breeders started to introduce other coat types to suit local conditions. For example, a dog with a wiry coat could work brambles, and a long-coated dog was better suited to withstand the elements.

The original Dachshunds were smooth-coated.

The long coat was obtained by breeding with a spaniel-type dog.

Long-haired

Long-haired Dachshunds were shown in Germany around 1883. Captain von Brunau was the first recorded breeder, and he stated that the Long-haired variety should have the same colours as the Smooth, but that the coat should be like that of the spaniel.

It is believed that this coat was obtained by breeding to the Wachtelhund, a small German spaniel-type dog, mostly used for quail-hunting.

Wire-haired

One of the first breeders of Wire-haired Dachshunds was Captain van Wardenburg of Hamburg, whose dogs were seen in the show ring in the early 1880s.

The Wire coat was developed by breeding Smooth Dachshunds with German Pinschers or Dandie Dinmont Terriers. Although the Dandie introduced some of the best characteristics of the terrier strain, it is also responsible for an occasional soft coat, which is sometimes a problem in Wire Dachshunds where a short, tough, coat is required.

SHOW VS. WORK

At the end of the 19th century, Dachshunds were the most popular breed at German dog shows. In addition to the parent club (the Teckel Klub), regional Dachshund clubs sprang up all over Germany.

There were many differences of opinion as to the virtues of the Dachshunds, and some characteristics began to be exaggerated, such as extreme length, deepness of chest, and crookedness of leg. To counter the trend, in 1910, the German Hunting Dachshunds Club was formed, and Field Trials were introduced to emphasise that the Dachshund was primarily a working dog.

Dogs successfully examined at these trials were given special numbers that were then added to their names. Dogs that had not been awarded working certificates were discouraged from being awarded prizes at shows. Today, most European countries still hold Field Trials for Dachshunds.

THE DACHSHUND IN BRITAIN

In the mid-18th century, a well-known importer of dogs, Mr Schuller from London, brought several hundred Dachshunds into Britain. Early prints of these first British Dachshunds show them to be much higher on the leg than today's dogs, and very crooked front legs seemed the norm (there was a theory that crooked legs were better for digging).

New Dachshund owners soon got bitten by the show bug, and the first representatives of the breed to win prizes at shows in England were Carl and Grete, bred in Germany by Count Knyphauser, and owned by Mr Corbet from Shropshire. Carl and Grete were shown at Birmingham in 1866, and were each awarded a prize in the 'Extra Class for any Known Breed of Sporting Dogs'.

Gernot vom Ludenbuhl: Imported from Germany by Madame Rikovsky.

Ch. Firs Cruiser: An early British Champion, bred from the early imported German stock.

The early exhibits were often described in show catalogues as German Badger Hounds and, in 1874, the Kennel Club, in the first issue of its Stud Book, recognised the breed and described them as 'Dachshunds (or German Badger Hounds)'.

These early exhibits were all Standard-sized and Smooth-haired – the Wires, the Long-hairs, and the Miniatures were yet to reach Britain. Very often, these early classes were separated by colour. In a 1874 show at Birmingham, two classes were given: one for red and one for 'other than red', and in 1875 at the Crystal Palace show, there were classes for black-and-tan and 'other than black-and-tan'.

At this Crystal Palace show, Prince Albert Solms judged the Dachshunds, and the Prince of Wales (later Edward VII) won first prize with his dog, Deurstich. The second prize winner was bred by Queen Victoria.

Royal Connections

As well as being a good hunting dog, the Dachshund also enjoyed a huge rise in popularity as a pet. This can be attributed to his international royal status. Many of the royal houses in Europe originated from Germany, and nearly all owned and bred Dachshunds.

In Britain, the Dachshund's rise to fame owes much to the marriage in 1840 of Prince Albert of Saxe-Coburg-Gotha to Queen Victoria. In addition to bringing his beloved Greyhound, Eos, to England with him, Prince Albert also brought two Dachshunds, and the breed has remained a favourite in the royal household up to the present day.

Queen Victoria became quite devoted to her Dachshunds and, when she was ill, there was usually a Dachshund in the bed with her. These early Dachshunds appear to have been bred by Prince Edward of Saxe-Weimar, and they were often used for hunting in Windsor Forest.

Many of the British aristocracy owned Dachshunds. Among the early names recorded were Lord Craven, the Earl of Onslow, and Lady Ker, as well as the Prince of Wales. Millais, the painter, owned and exhibited Dachshunds, and Matthew Arnold, the poet, was a dedicated Dachshund owner all his life, writing numerous poems in their honour.

First UK Club

On January 17th 1881, Major Harry Jones, the Reverend G.F. Lovell, William Arkright and Montague Wooten met in Cox's Hotel in Jermyn Street, London, and the Dachshund Club was founded.

William Arkwright was interested in most sporting dogs, and Major Harry Jones had many Dachshunds; he was the proud owner and breeder of Jackdaw, who was born in 1886 out of Wagtail by Charkov. This dog was to become a legend in the breed, and was never beaten in his show career.

Reverend Lovell owned several winning imported Dachshunds, some of which, depicted in old prints, look as though they could hold their own in the ring today. Major Jones was elected the first president of the club, and Montague Wooten the first secretary.

Outbreak Of War

Kaiser Wilhelm II, the Emperor of Germany and King of Prussia during World War I, had always been a devoted Dachshund lover. He was seldom seen without at least one at his feet, even when reviewing his troops. They appeared at every royal function, and they were described as being nearer to the Kaiser than all his faithful servants.

On one famous occasion in Berlin in 1893, when all the grand company was assembled to await their majesties for a formal breakfast, the door was suddenly flung open. The company arose, but, instead of the royal family, a horde of little Dachshunds rushed in. They had a wonderful time, barking and leaping all over the guests, nipping at silken legs and grabbing anything at hand, and no one dared stop them. When the Kaiser did eventually appear, he stood

The outbreak of war resulted in troubled times for the Dachshund.

The Long-haired variety was the last to arrive in Britain.

and eyed the scene. "Oh, you bad boys," he said, laughing, and left them to continue their fun.

Sadly, the fact that Dachshunds were so closely associated with Germany in their early history was to lead to a traumatic period in their rise to fame in Britain and also in the United States. During World War I, Dachshunds were stoned in the streets and anyone seen with one was often jeered at, so that it became dangerous to take them anywhere.

Coat Varieties

In the breed's early days, only Smooth Dachshunds were recorded in Britain, but soon a few Wires began to appear. At Guildford, Surrey, in 1894, there was a class for 'rough-coated', which was won by Woolsack.

Wires had been especially popular in Germany with the foresters because they were bolder and tougher (owing to their German Pinscher ancestry), and the foresters found them excellent at hunting and tracking the fierce wild boar.

The last of the three coats to arrive in Britain was the Long-haired. This variety started to appear around 1920, but it took ten years to achieve full recognition.

The Minis Arrive

Miniature Dachshunds were very popular in Germany from the beginning of the breed's history, but there does not seem to be any mention of them in Britain until after World War I, when a few started to be imported from Germany.

The Miniature Dachshund Club was formed in 1935, and the dogs were granted Championship status in 1959. The first Mini to become a Champion was a little bitch, Ch. Jane of Sillwood, owned by Mrs Wakefield.

THE AMERICAN DACHSHUND

The history of the Dachshund in America began in the mid-19th century, spearheaded by a few dedicated enthusiasts.

Some early imports came from Britain, but the majority came from Germany. Many dogs were imported by German immigrants who were still in close contact with their homeland. Two of the very earliest recorded Dachshunds were Caesar and Minka; both were black-and-tan Smooths and they were owned by a Mr Fleischmann, who used them with great success to hunt woodchucks in the mountains.

The first few Dachshunds were registered in America between 1879 and 1885, and by 1885 they had become so popular that the Dachshund Club of America was founded, followed by many regional clubs.

The imports to the United States were of the finest quality, from the most famous winning kennels, including those belonging to Major Ilgner, the Duke of Coburg, and the Count of Bismarck.

Before the Dachshund was officially recognised by the American Kennel Club, the early pioneers had a struggle to get their dogs entered at shows. One of the very earliest recorded winners was a red dog named Unser Fritz, bred in Germany by the Duke of Baden, and owned by a Dr Traddell.

Fall And Rise

During the 1914-1918 war, as in Britain, anti-German mania was rife, and so the poor Teckel suffered. Many famous kennels were forced to disband, and owners were even reported to have shot all their dogs for fear of persecution. Because of its Germanic-sounding name, 'Dachshund' was dropped by the American Kennel Club and replaced by 'Badger Hound'. Happily, by 1923, the word 'Dachshund' was reinstated in catalogues and pedigrees, and the breed's popularity as a loyal companion was fully restored.

When the Dachshund was adopted by some of the big Hollywood stars, such as Clark Gable and Noel Coward, its future was assured.

Registrations continued to rise from almost none during the war years, until 48,569 Dachshunds (of all coats and sizes) were registered at the American Kennel Club by 1964. The breed has gone from strength to strength, and continues to be one of the most popular purebred dogs registered with the American Kennel Club.

WORLDWIDE POPULARITY

Today, the Dachshund is a popular breed all over Europe and far beyond. The Wires are particularly strong in Sweden, where they are called Taxen. The Danes love the Dachshund too, calling him Gravhund (Earth Dog), and in Poland, he is known as Jamnik (Hole Dog).

' Fortunately the breed's popularity was restored '

In the early days, the French called them Bassets de Race Allemande, but today they are Teckels or Dachshunds. In South Africa, where all Dachshund varieties are very popular, he is referred to (unofficially) as the Worsie, meaning Little Sausage!

A BREED APART

Whatever his name, the Dachshund, with the variety of sizes, coat types and colours to choose from, is a welcome addition to most homes. However, the Dachshund is no lapdog. You must be prepared for a strong, sometimes wilful, character, whose working instincts are never too far from the fore – particularly when it comes to digging holes in your beautifully manicured lawn! Read on to find out more.

CHAPTER TWO

PUPPY POWER

Miniature or Standard, Smooth, Wire, or Long-coated, the Dachshund is a breed that inspires great enthusiasm. However, before taking the plunge into ownership, you must consider the long-term commitment involved in looking after a Dachshund, a breed that can live well into its middle teens.

Puppies are hard work, requiring considerable time and commitment: an eight-week-old needs to be fed four times a day, so there must be someone at home to see to this and to house-train him, too.

Adult Dachsies are no pushover, either. They require a minimum of two 20-minute walks a day, whatever the weather. They need training, veterinary care, regular grooming, and heaps of love. They must not be left at home alone all day long (never longer than four hours) so, if you work full-time, you must make arrange-ments for a responsible person to dog-sit.

Your freedom will also be restricted for the next 15 years or so. You won't be able to drop everything suddenly and dash off somewhere for the weekend. You will have to check first whether you can take the dog, or arrange for a dog-sitter or a boarding kennel.

Your bank balance will be severely affected too. Owning a dog can be an expensive business – the initial outlay on a bed, crate, lead and collar, bowls, toys, and so on is bad enough, but it is nothing compared with the long-term food, veterinary, and grooming bills that will be incurred.

If you are absolutely certain you can meet all these responsibilities, then read on.

DO YOUR HOMEWORK

Before you embark on your quest for the perfect puppy, it is essential to research the breed thoroughly – read books, look on the Internet, and talk to as many Dachshund owners as you can. Contact your national kennel club too, which will be able to put you in contact with Dachshund breed clubs. Club members will be happy to chat to you about the breed.

CHOOSING A TYPE

Once you are sure the Dachshund is the dog for you, it is time to decide on the coat type and size. There are six types of Dachshund in Britain and the United States – Long-haired, Smooth-haired, and Wire-haired, in Standard and Miniature sizes. Germany has nine types, as it also has the Kaninchenteckel, an even smaller size than the Miniature.

The size you choose is really dependent on your personal preference. A Miniature may be better if you live in an apartment or a small house.

Standard Wire (left) and Mini Wire: You will need to choose coat type and size, bearing in mind differences in temperament between the varieties.

The different Dachshund varieties should really be considered as separate breeds, as each one has its own characteristics and temperament.

For example, a Miniature Smooth isn't simply a smaller version of the Standard; often he is more vocal and bossy than his larger cousin. Talk to as many breeders as you can, to find out the different characteristics of the types (they may vary between countries and between pedigree lines).

If you are lucky, you may find a Dachshund breeder who is not too far from your home, so you can visit the dogs. You may locate a breeder who has both Standard and Miniature sizes and possibly some different coat varieties, and this will give you an opportunity to assess all the different breed types.

Experiencing the breed first-hand, assessing temperament and seeing the different coat types, is very important – after all, one of these dogs will be sharing your home with you for a long time to come.

Smooth-haired

Both sizes are affectionate, and make excellent family pets, as long as they are brought up with children from the start.

Some Smooths seem to be a little more timid than other Dachshund coat types, but thorough socialisation and training during puppyhood overcomes this.

The Smooth coat is by far the easiest to look after, simply requiring a good brushing once a week (see page 61).

You will need to enjoy grooming if you opt for a Long-haired Dachshund.

The Long-haired coat needs far more attention. These dogs are the most glamorous of the three coat varieties, but will need grooming at least two or three times a week. However, the grooming needn't be bothersome, as long as you maintain a regular, thorough grooming routine (see page 61).

Wire-haired

Along with having a terrier-type coat, the Wire-haired has a very terrier-like character, and is usually more feisty, tenacious and spirited than the other Dachshund types.

This coat needs to be trimmed or stripped out, and the breeders of this variety will be happy to give you advice on this procedure (see page 61).

Long-haired

The Long-haired Dachshund loves human company. Although he looks glamorous, he doesn't need – or want – to be mollycoddled, and is much more laid-back and robust than his looks suggest.

Coat Colours

The Dachshund comes in a wide variety of colours and markings:
• Red

Dapples are not so easy to find.

A chocolate-coloured Dachshund.

- Shaded red (mixture of black hair interspersed in the red usually along the back, on the tail, and on the ears)
- Black
- Chocolate
- Grey (blue)
- Fawn (Isabella)
- Wild boar (brown or grey with a black stripe down the back, and brindled sides)
- Brindle (striped).

There are also two-colour Dachshunds, which have tan markings on their coats, the most popular of which is the black-and-tan combination.

The striking dappled coat is another popular choice with pet owners.

- Chocolate dapple (the base colour of the coat is chocolate, with silver-white hairs interspersed in it, overlaid with patches of chocolate).
- Silver dapple (silver-grey base colour, interspersed with black and white hair, with black patches distributed through the coat).

- Red dapple (red base colour, interspersed with red and white hairs through the coat, overlaid with solid red patches).

With so much choice, there's a Dachshund to suit everyone's colour preferences!

IDEAL TYPE

Within the different varieties of Dachshund, there is diversity of type – not all Standard Wires look the same, do they? To ascertain the type you prefer, visit some dog shows (advertised in dog publications). There, you will be able to see lots of different Dachshunds and have a chance to speak to the owners after they have finished in the ring. Try to find out about their dogs, and ask as many questions as you can to see if they have a long-standing knowledge of the breed. If they don't have a litter for sale, they may be able to recommend someone who has.

MALE OR FEMALE?

Finally you should decide whether you want a male or a female. Both sexes make great family dogs, so this is really a matter of personal choice.

With a female, you must consider that she will come 'in season' every six months or so. The season lasts about three weeks and the middle week is when the bitch will accept the attentions of a male, so this is the time you need to be vigilant – or you will end up with a litter of unplanned puppies. Sensible precautions taken by the owner during this time can eliminate the possibility of 'unwelcome male callers', as well as

Do your homework, and find a breeder who has a reputation for producing good-quality stock.

taking the steps to keep the bitch at home for the duration of her season.

Being a small breed, Dachshunds do not make a lot of mess when in season, and usually keep themselves very clean.

However, if you have a female and don't intend to breed from her, it is wise to have her spayed. This will stop the inconvenience of coping with her seasons, and will also prevent her from developing certain life-threatening conditions, such as pyometra.

Males are less trouble in that you don't have seasons to worry about, but they may wander after females in the neighbourhood if your garden is not as secure as it should be. They can be castrated to prevent this testosterone-induced wanderlust, and, as with spaying, castration confers several health benefits, such as eliminating the risk of prostate disorders. Your vet will be happy to give you more details about spaying and neutering.

See Chapter Four for more information on neutering.

FINDING A BREEDER

Now that you know exactly what Dachshund you want – coat, size, colour, type, and sex – it is time to find an experienced, reputable breeder. The starting point is your national kennel club, who will give you details of breed clubs, which, in turn, can put you in contact with breeders.

The majority of breeders produce well-bred, well-reared puppies, but there are exceptions, so be careful. Take note of word-of-mouth recommendations from breed club members, and you should also ask the following:

• Have the litter's parents been health-screened for any problems within that variety of Dachshund (ask your vet for details)?

• Will the breeder take the puppy back if you have any problems? Make sure the terms and conditions of the sale are written down.

• Will the breeder give after-sales advice for the entire life of the pup?

Home-reared

A home-reared litter is generally preferable to

Ask to see the mother of the puppies so you can assess her temperament as well as her looks.

with you. Dachshunds are naturally inquisitive and will rummage through your handbag or your pockets, if they get half a chance. While the dogs get to know you, take the opportunity to see if they all look healthy and well cared for.

Make a mental note of the environment, and check that the premises are clean. Ask to see the mother of the litter and assess her temperament as well as her physical wellbeing. The puppy could well turn out to be like his mother – would you be happy for this to happen?

Happy And Healthy

Always look for a healthy, playful puppy with a shiny coat, good body covering, and clear, bright eyes. In most cases, a young puppy with a 'pot-belly' is not an indication of a well-fed puppy – rather, it could indicate a worm infestation. Check with the breeder that the puppy has been wormed regularly.

A puppy with cloudy or runny eyes is also something to watch for, as it could suggest that the puppy may be becoming ill.

A puppy's temperament is one of the most important things to consider, as he is likely to take his basic character with him into adulthood. Puppies should be lively and playful. Beware of the subdued puppy that is not keen to play or join in with his littermates. This could be an indication of poor health or a suspect temperament.

Do not pick the shy, timid puppy out of pity, as it will probably grow up to be nervous. This type of puppy is best suited to an experienced owner who knows how to handle him. A shy

one raised in a kennel unless you find a breeder who works very hard at early socialisation. Puppies who have lived in a home will be used to all the usual comings and goings of home life. They will be familiar with everyday sounds, such as the washing machine or the vacuum cleaner. They will also have enjoyed more contact with people, and therefore will settle more quickly into their new homes.

SELECTING A PUPPY

When you visit a litter, don't rush into buying the first pup you see. Remember, this puppy will be a member of your family for a long time to come, so don't settle for the first pretty face you see. If you are lucky enough to have found a couple of litters, take your time and visit them both.

Visiting the litter will be a good opportunity to meet the breeder's adult dogs. Be warned: Dachshunds bark on first introductions (and, for little dogs, they have big barks!), but then they will settle down and set about making friends

Watch the puppies playing together and you will see their personalities begin to emerge.

pup can still make a loving pet, but needs more intensive, sensitive handling to bring him out of his shell.

OLDER DOGS

Never rule out having an older dog as a pet. Sometimes, a retired show dog that has finished breeding can make a loyal and devoted companion and would probably not cost as much as a puppy. An adult that is already trained and socialised will be less demanding than a puppy. However, do make sure that your

home circumstances are as close as possible to those that he is already used to. For example, it is unfair to expect an adult dog to come into a house full of kids when he has led a quiet life in the past.

Sometimes, you may be offered an older puppy of about four to five months. This puppy may have been one that the breeder had been observing to decide whether he is suitable for the show ring. In this case, you could be getting 'second pick of the litter' at a pet price.

A rescued Dachshund is another consideration – see Chapter Five.

ASSESSING SHOW POTENTIAL

If you would like to show your Dachshund in the future, take the advice of the puppy's breeder. He or she will probably keep the best example, but may be able to advise you on other potential show puppies in the litter.

You should look for a well-balanced pup that is typical of the breed.

'Long, low and level' is a term used for Dachshunds, but this can become exaggerated if you are not careful – too long and too low is a fault which has been depicted by cartoonists over the years and has ended up with the noble breed being nicknamed 'sausage dogs'.

As with a pet puppy, you should also look for a healthy, outgoing dog with lots of character. A show dog should have a real presence in the ring, and should thrive when he is the centre of attention. He should also move with style, and carry his head well.

Do remember, however, that show potential is

When assessing show potential, look for a balanced puppy, with no exaggerated features, that thrives on being the centre of attention.

never a guarantee of show success, and your puppy may not develop into the show star you hoped for.

PRE-PUP PREPARATIONS

There are a number of items that you should buy in readiness for bringing home your Dachshund puppy. Ask the breeder what food the puppy is used to, so that you can buy in some supplies beforehand. For your training sessions, you should buy a soft, light lead and collar. For his beauty bag, your pup will need a brush, comb, toothbrush, doggie meat-flavoured toothpaste, and guillotine-type nail clippers.

An indoor crate will be the most expensive outlay, but it will be invaluable for the dog's entire life (see page 27). When not being used as your dog's sleeping area, it can be used in the car, or when visiting friends. Make sure it is large enough to accommodate your Dachshund when he is fully grown, and that he will have plenty of space to move around comfortably.

A stair-gate is another must. These portable gates fit across the stairs to bar the puppy's access. No breed of puppy should be allowed to climb the stairs while their bones are growing, but it is particularly important when dealing with the short-legged, long-backed Dachshund who can sustain serious damage through such energetic exertions.

You might also like to consider putting small ramps or steps around the house, so your Dachshund will never need to jump up or down. For example, if your Dachshund will be allowed on to the sofa, put a small step (such as a large book) on the floor so he can reach the sofa with ease. (This is particularly useful with older dogs that may be a little arthritic too.)

Safe chew toys should also feature on your list. It is natural for puppies to chew, and, if you don't want your shoes or sofa to be victims of

An indoor crate can be used in the house, and also when you go out in the car.

his chomping, you should provide your pup with something suitable to satisfy his craving. Rope toys are particularly good. Be wary of cheap plastic toys that may not be able to withstand a puppy's chewing. They may fragment into small pieces that can be swallowed, causing serious injury and possible death. Check toys regularly, and replace them if there are any signs of damage.

Safety First

Before you bring home your Dachshund puppy, make sure that your home and garden are puppy-proofed. It is amazing how much damage a puppy can wreak, so remove anything that you don't want to be destroyed, or that could be dangerous for the puppy.

Move everything out of the puppy's reach – electrical cables, ornaments, shoes, anything that is hazardous or that you would be upset to lose. Don't underestimate the level of destruction a puppy can achieve – chewing, smashing, scratching or urinating destroys most things eventually!

Your garden should also be assessed for possible danger. Keep your garden tools safely shut away, and do not use any pesticides (e.g. slug pellets) that are toxic to dogs. Check that the plants in your garden are also safe, as they are likely to be nibbled by your pup. Your garden centre should be able to advise you. Also, be sure that your garden fencing is secure. Dachshunds are born to dig, so make sure the fence foundations are deep, or your pup could tunnel his way out.

Dachshund puppies can sniff out mischief, so make sure your garden is safe and secure.

Veterinary Care

Before bringing your Dachshund home, you should register him with a nearby veterinary surgery. If you have never owned a pet before, ask the advice of the breeder (if he or she is local) or chat with dog-owning friends who may be able to recommend a vet. Make an appointment with the surgery for the day after you bring home your Dachshund so that he can be checked over. Remember to take details of any treatments, such as worming, that your puppy has received.

Health Insurance

In Britain, many breeders insure the puppies before they leave for their new homes, and the cover usually lasts for four to six weeks. Pet

IDENTITY CHECK

It is important that your Dachshund is identified, in case he should become lost. A collar tag, engraved with your details, can be purchased from most pet stores or vet practices. However, it is important to have a belt-and-braces approach, and to consider permanently microchipping your Dachshund too, as identification in the event of him losing his collar or tag.

A microchip is the size of a long grain of rice, and is inserted between the shoulder blades by a vet. When scanned with a special reader, it provides all the dog's contact details. Ask your vet for more details.

insurance is also available in the United States, although it is not as prevalent. It is certainly worth considering insuring your Dachshund once this temporary cover expires. Veterinary treatment is improving all the time, and diagnoses and treatments unheard of a few years ago are now commonplace. Veterinary specialists are available in a wide range of disciplines, but they can be costly. Having the protection of insurance means that you will not have to worry should the unexpected occur. Shop around to find the best policy. Remember that vaccinations, prophylactic dentistry, and other routine treatments are usually excluded.

HOMEWARD BOUND

Once all your pre-pup preparations are done, it won't be long before the big day arrives and it is time to collect your new Dachshund. Try to arrange to get the puppy in the morning so that you will have plenty of time to travel home and get to know each other before nightfall.

Before you take the puppy home, make sure the breeder gives you details of any veterinary treatments the puppy has received (worming dates and dosage, any vaccinations etc.), together with a diet sheet.

Trying to console a homesick pup while driving is not recommended, so ask a friend or family member to drive. You can then hold the puppy on your lap (protected by a soft towel in case of accidents), and concentrate on comforting him.

If it is a warm day, make sure there is plenty of ventilation and shade in the car. Take a supply of fresh water for the puppy to drink if you have a long journey.

At last, it is time to take your puppy home.

Home Sweet Home

When you arrive home, take your puppy outside to the garden to stretch his legs, sniff around, and to relieve himself. Then take him indoors so he can investigate further. Introduce him to the rest of the family, whether human, canine, or feline (pages 31, 33 and 35), keeping all meetings calm and quiet. The puppy is likely to be a little nervous of this new environment, and you don't want him thinking he has moved into a madhouse – not until he is settled, anyway!

After all the excitement, the puppy will need to catch up on his sleep. Although it may seem as if they never rest, puppies do need lots of sleep. Like babies, sleep is vital to their growth and wellbeing, so make sure your Dachshund is taken to his bed for naps throughout the day.

Great Crates

A crate is an ideal place for your Dachshund to snatch 40 winks. Filled with comfortable bedding and a couple of safe chews and toys, your puppy will regard it as a palace.

Make sure the family understands that the pup must not be disturbed while he is in his crate – he should learn that it is his own little spot in the house where he can retire if he wants a nap.

Never put the puppy in his crate as a punishment, or for long periods of time. At night, while the family sleeps, he can be kept in the crate, as no one will be able to supervise him and he could get into all sorts of mischief or danger. However, the crate is not a replacement dog-sitter – it is completely unacceptable to leave your Dachshund in the crate for eight

Your puppy will soon learn to settle when he is left at night.

hours while you go to work. It should only be used for short periods – for an hour while you go shopping, for example, or if you have visitors who dislike dogs.

Bedtime Blues

Just before settling your puppy into bed for the night, take him outside to relieve himself. Put him in his crate (or in a dog-proofed room), and do not return to him until the early morning, when you should take him outside again.

Do not expect to get too much sleep during the puppy's first night. He will be in unfamiliar surroundings, alone for the first time in his life, away from his mother, littermates, and from human companionship.

So how should you react if your pup starts howling or barking? You should stay away from him – no matter what. A young puppy's cry sounds incredibly pitiful, but do not give in, or the puppy will learn that you come whenever he calls.

If the puppy learns, right from the start, that his barking is in vain, he will stop – what's the point of doing something that does not elicit a response? So be prepared to sacrifice a few nights of sleep at the beginning – it will be worth it in the long run. Meanwhile, invest in some ear plugs and a good book to get you through.

FEEDING

The breeder should have given you a diet sheet when you collected your puppy – and this should be followed to the letter, at least for the first week or so. Change and excitement can cause upset stomachs in young puppies. With the move to his new home, your Dachshund is experiencing enough upheaval and does not need to cope with a change in diet too.

Changing Diet

After a couple of weeks, once your Dachshund has settled into his new home, you can think about changing his diet, if it is not suitable. Replacing one food with another should be done very gradually. Add a little of the new food to the puppy's current food, and gradually add more, over the course of a week or so. Each time you give more of one food, put in less of the other, until, eventually, a complete changeover has been achieved.

Number Of Meals

When you take your puppy home at around eight weeks of age, he will need four meals a day. Your puppy's breeder will tell you what – and how much – to feed (remember: Miniatures require only half the amounts needed by Standards).

Around the age of 12 weeks, your puppy will probably start leaving one of his meals, usually his lunch or his supper. This meal can then be removed, with the size of the other three meals increased accordingly. If your puppy doesn't leave any food, then remove one meal, as convenient. If he won't settle for the night without his supper, then give a small meal, late evening, before he goes to bed.

Another meal can go when the puppy is around eight or nine months old. You can then continue to feed a morning and evening meal for the rest of the dog's life, or you can cut down to one meal a day when your dog is 12 months old. Tip: most Dachshunds are real 'foodies' and prefer to have two meals a day.

It is imperative to stick to regular mealtimes. Leaving food down all the time is not only unhygienic, but it tends to nurture picky eaters.

Types Of Food

Complete foods are growing in popularity. They are nutritionally complete, containing all the

HEALTHY APPETITE

It is rare to find a Dachshund that does not lick his bowl clean every mealtime.

If your Dachshund puppy is off his food, you should get him checked over by a vet, as a health problem could be causing his lack of appetite.

Puppies are used to competing for their food among their littermates.

vitamins and minerals a growing puppy needs, and in the right quantity. They are easy to store, and are clean and simple to feed.

Most complete food brands have different life stages, providing food for the puppy, adult, working dog, and senior, so you can be sure your Dachshund is being provided with the right balance of nutrients all through his life – without you having to do all the calculations and cooking.

Canned dog foods are another option. They can be fed with dry meal, and are enjoyed by most dogs.

Fresh water should always be available to your Dachshund puppy – this is especially important if you are feeding a dry, complete diet.

Home-made diets, particularly those based on raw food, are becoming increasingly popular. In theory, they work well – providing only fresh, wholesome ingredients every mealtime. However, these diets are best avoided unless you

are totally confident that you are supplying all the nutritional needs of a puppy, and are able to prepare fresh food every mealtime. It is very easy to undernourish your Dachshund in certain vitamins and minerals unless you have a complete understanding of a dog's nutritional requirements.

If you are adamant that you would like to pursue this option, you must first discuss your growing puppy's dietary needs with your vet.

Healthy Eating

Never get into the habit of feeding fatty, sugary foods to your puppy. Dachshunds are prone to put on weight, but their frames cannot tolerate obesity at all, so give your Dachsie a raw carrot rather than a biscuit when giving treats, or he will grow up to have a sweet tooth. Wholewheat bread crusts, cut into small pieces and dried, make good, crunchy treats if he does not like carrots.

CHAPTER THREE

EARLY LESSONS

The first few months of having a puppy can be exhausting. There's so much to remember, such as numerous feeds, taking the puppy out regularly, early training, and intensive socialisation. But, if you organise a routine, where you put all the things you need to do in a timetable, it will all go much more smoothly, and will help the puppy to settle too.

FIRST IMPRESSIONS COUNT

CHILD'S PLAY

The majority of children, especially younger ones, love animals, and having a pet can be an important learning experience for them. Involving children in caring for the family pet not only teaches them the responsibilities and commitment of keeping an animal, but also teaches the puppy how to behave around children.

Before you bring home the Dachshund puppy, you should have already set the ground rules, which the children should be familiar with. For example, if you have decided that the puppy is not allowed on the furniture, then the children should be told not to encourage the puppy to jump up for a sneaky cuddle. Whatever your rules are, inform the family, and all stick to them!

Even if you don't have children in the home, it is essential to socialise your puppy with them. Borrow nieces and nephews, grandchildren, or friends' children, so your puppy has contact with them early on. A dog that is unfamiliar with children can grow up to be wary of them – and may lash out through fear if he feels threatened, so a few hours spent on supervised introductions is well worth the time and effort.

Play-time

Puppies and children often become firm friends. However, both should be taught to play gently, and not to get too overexcited. Here are some

Supervise play sessions to make sure the puppy does not get too excited.

general rules:
- Running around with the puppy is not acceptable – it won't be long before the pup is squashed underfoot in all the excitement.
- Picking up the puppy should also be forbidden. The puppy could be dropped by accident, and could be seriously injured.
- Biting is never acceptable. As soon as the puppy chews or mouths a child (or any human), the 'victim' should squeal loudly, then turn or walk away from the puppy. Puppies love attention, and hate being ignored, so this is the best way to teach your pup that biting will not be tolerated.

Training Respect

It is important that your Dachshund puppy learns to respect children, as well as seeing them as playmates. This is best achieved by involving children in the puppy's training.

Follow the basic training exercises on pages 42 to 47, and once you have laid the early foundations, enlist the help of a whole range of people, including children, to continue with the exercises. This will teach the puppy that he must obey everyone, and with this understanding comes respect for people, regardless of their age, sex, or size.

Incorporate the exercises into the puppy's everyday routines. For example, teach the puppy to Sit before he is given his food bowl. Different members of the family should practise this exercise to help the pup to understand that obedience is expected of him 24 hours a day, not simply during his training sessions.

Feeding

One of the quickest ways to earn a Dachshund's respect is through his stomach! Renowned for their love of food, Dachshunds will quickly become bonded to anyone who feeds them.
- While your Dachshund is still young, it is helpful to have a child periodically give the puppy his meals.
- If the puppy attempts to jump up or snaps, the child should tell him "No" firmly, and should command him to "Sit". Only when he is sitting quietly should he be given his meal.
- A couple of times throughout the puppy's meal, the child should take the bowl away for just long enough to put in a tasty treat, such as a small piece of cheese, sausage, or liver (something tastier than his usual food).

Drop a couple of treats into the feed, and then the puppy will not become possessive over his food bowl.

- If the puppy growls or jumps up to get his bowl back, he should be told to "Sit", and should be given the bowl only when he is sitting quietly.
- This exercise should be repeated at least once a week during the puppy's first six months or so, and then periodically thereafter.
- This exercise should prevent your Dachshund from becoming possessive of his bowl. Far from fearing that his food is being taken away from him, he will realise that something tasty is always given.

FELINE INTRODUCTIONS

Cats are great survivors, and adapt to most situations. They may not be overjoyed to have a puppy in the house, especially one as playful as a Dachshund, but they will soon learn to cope, especially if they learn that the puppy is not a great threat.

- Put the puppy in his crate, so that your curious cat will be able to sniff him and investigate safely. A few meetings like this will increase their familiarity, and the novelty of seeing each other will soon wear off.
- Take your puppy out of his crate for the next meeting, and put him on a lead. Let the cat and puppy sniff each other out. If either gets too exuberant, say "No!" firmly. They must be taught to respect each other.
- If the cat wishes to escape, let her. Most will opt for an upward escape route – such as a shelf or a windowsill – where they can scrutinise the puppy, while safely out of reach.
- Increased exposure to each other (always supervised) will make them more comfortable, so short, frequent meetings should be organised. Always end the sessions with a tasty treat for both pets, so they learn to associate cats/puppies with enjoyable experiences.

If care is taken, Dachshunds and cats can learn to live in harmony.

CANINE INTRODUCTIONS

Bringing a puppy into the home of another dog should be handled sensitively. The resident dog will view his home as his castle – his own territory – and it may be unnerving for him to have to face a bouncy, lively little puppy that is unpredictable and seems to have no respect for his elders. This is the key. Your puppy should be taught that he is submissive to the older dog, who deserves deference and respect. The older dog should have certain privileges for his superior position; he should be allowed to go through doors before the other dog, for example, and should be allowed to discipline the puppy (within reason) if he oversteps the mark.

Provided your Dachshund puppy is duly respectful of the older dog (and most are), it won't be long before he becomes firm friends with the older dog. Many adult dogs enjoy a new lease of life when they have a puppy to play with – and you may find you suddenly have two pups to cope with!

First Meeting

The first meeting should be on territory that is as neutral as possible. If you have taken on an older Dachshund, or a puppy that has had its full course of vaccinations, a park would be an ideal spot. If you have an eight-week-old puppy, introductions will have to be carried out in your garden.

Allow them to sniff noses, and then let them get to know each other. Supervise them, but don't interfere. Dogs are very social animals, with a unique system of communicating

Dachshunds enjoy each other's company, but make sure you are tactful when the new puppy arrives home.

through sound and body language. Your puppy will have practised his 'vocabulary' from playing with his mother and littermates, so he will be able to communicate with the older dog. For example, if he gets too overexcited when he plays, the older dog will tell him so and the puppy will learn to curb his exuberance.

Try not to get involved – unless there is a real danger to the pup's safety. Interfering unnecessarily could be confusing, and might undermine the older dog's superior status over the puppy.

If your puppy has any sense about him, he will soon lie on his back, exposing his belly. This submissive gesture shows that the puppy respects the older dog's seniority.

GREEN-EYED MONSTERS

When a new puppy arrives, it is a great temptation to spend all your time with him, excluding your resident pets. This will not go unnoticed, and there is a danger that your other pets may resent the new addition to the family, seeing him as a rival for your affections. Set aside some quality time to spend alone with your dog, or cat, when the puppy is asleep in his crate, or being looked after in another part of the house. This reaffirmation of your affection for your other pets will help to reduce any tension, and should help achieve household harmony.

HOUSE RULES

As previously mentioned, it is very important to sit down, as a family, and discuss the puppy's house rules, before you bring home your Dachshund. It is even more important that they be implemented consistently, from the first moment the puppy arrives home. Every home is different, but here are some rules you may wish to consider:

• NO BEGGING

Dachshunds are typical hounds. They can sniff out food from great distances, and have rehearsed the most heart-melting expression in their begging routines. Everyone in your family will have to learn to become hardened against those big, beautiful eyes, which can be very persuasive!

Be warned: if someone gives a Dachshund only one treat from the table, he will always remember it and will continue to beg just in case someone gives in again. Ask all visitors not to feed the dog from the table, or all your hard work will go to waste – solidarity is essential!

It is important for your puppy to understand what is acceptable behaviour.

• NO BED-SHARING

Although they are quite tough dogs, designed for outdoor work, Dachshunds do also like their creature comforts. Given the chance, they would happily spend every night cuddled up with you in your bed. They can even use their burrowing skills to tunnel under the covers for the very warmest spot. For the first few nights, while your puppy is small, this may be endearing. However, if you let your Dachshund share your bed once, he will forever think it his right. Are you prepared to continue sharing your bed with a much larger, adult Dachshund?

Also be warned that sharing your bed can send out different signals to your dog, who may see it as a sign of his elevated status in the family 'pack'. It's fine if your Dachsie views you as pack leader and obeys you unquestioningly, jumping off the bed when you ask him to. However, if he starts to grumble when you ask him to move, then you have a problem, which could have been avoided by not letting him on the bed (or on the sofa) in the first place.

• NO BARKING

Hounds are barkers, and the Dachshund is no exception. Barking is a natural canine communication, and you should not attempt to stop your dog from barking altogether. That would be cruel and unnatural. However, you want to teach your puppy that excessive barking is not acceptable.

For example, one or two warning barks when someone knocks at the door is fine. Prolonged frenzied barking, which continues long after the visitor is invited indoors, is not acceptable.

If your puppy barks inappropriately, tell him, calmly but firmly, "Quiet". Do not scream and shout – it will sound like barking to your puppy and he will join in. Ignore the puppy, perhaps putting him in another room. Let him out only when he is quiet. The visitor can then give the puppy a treat, so he learns to welcome people coming to the house.

See also Chapter Four.

• NO JUMPING UP

Visitors should not be 'mugged' on arrival. Being a low breed, the Dachshund often feels ignored and jumps up to alert people to his presence. This is a habit that your Dachshund should not be allowed to get into. It will be a real nuisance when he is older, bigger, has dirty, wet paws, or when he has just laddered yet another pair of tights, or ruined an umpteenth pair of trousers. Nip this behaviour in the bud while the puppy is still young.

As soon as your Dachsie jumps up at someone, he should be ignored at once. Turn away from him, and do not even look at him. Petting him, or even shouting at him, will only teach him that he gets attention – a reward – for jumping up. Puppies hate to be ignored, so this is the quickest way of teaching that jumping up is not acceptable. As soon as the puppy sits quietly, he can be petted.

> ❛ Hounds are barkers, and Dachshunds are no exception ❜

Encourage your pup to spend short periods in his crate so that he learns not to fear being left alone.

TIME ALONE

Your Dachshund puppy must get used to being away from his owners. If you are at home all day, the puppy will get used to being with you constantly, and may not be able to cope when he is eventually left, even for short periods. Right from the start, it is advisable to teach the puppy to be happy alone. That way, he will not be upset if someone else needs to dog-sit if you need to spend time in hospital, or go away on holiday.

A crate is ideal for helping to prevent separation anxiety. Your puppy should already see his crate as his comfortable little den, so he should feel safe and secure when spending time there.

- Put your puppy in his crate with some safe chew toys.
- Close the crate door and leave the room for a

couple of minutes, only returning to the puppy if he is not barking. If he is calling for you, wait until he is quiet before reappearing or he will learn that you come whenever he barks.

- Over the next few weeks, increase the length of time you stay away, until, eventually, the puppy can be left for a couple of hours.

Always toilet your pup before putting him in the crate, and never make a big deal about leaving. Do not say goodbye or cuddle him, or the puppy will get excited, and will miss you even more when you are gone. Equally, never make a fuss when you return. Maybe give him a treat, but be quiet and calm. This avoids the puppy getting too excited in anticipation of your return.

PUPPY CARE

GROOMING

Unless you have a Smooth-coated Dachshund, you are likely to spend many, many hours over the next 15 years or so with a brush in your hand. A puppy coat is quite easy to care for, but it is advisable to get your Dachshund used to grooming while he is still young in order to avoid tantrums and struggles when he is older. Make grooming an enjoyable experience. Brush the puppy gently, and give treats intermittently throughout the grooming session, as a reward for being well behaved.

TOUCH SENSITIVITY

It is also useful to get the puppy accustomed to

having his paws and ears touched. This will make life much easier when you come to clip his nails when he is older, inspect his feet after a walk, or check his ears. As Dachshunds have pendulous ears, they can be prone to ear infections, so routine checks are important.

When the puppy is relaxed, following one of his grooming sessions, gently touch his feet and massage his ears. Give a treat while you do this. Keep the sessions short to begin with, so he doesn't become bored or restless. Gradually progress to lifting up his ears to check inside (see page 64).

During teething (from 12 to 20 weeks of age), some puppies can develop sore ears, so be particularly vigilant at this time, and seek veterinary advice if you have any concerns.

If the puppy's nails are too long, they will need clipping. When your puppy visits the vet to have his vaccinations, you can ask your vet to show you how to do this.

EXERCISE

Dachshund puppies are as curious as their adult counterparts. Nose to the ground, they will want to follow different scents and investigate their surroundings. It is important, however, not to overexercise your Dachshund. Yes, it is a good way of tiring him out, but you could unwittingly be causing permanent skeletal and joint problems. Exercise should be increased very gradually during the puppy's growing period, so as not to cause undue stress to his body.

Until your Dachshund is vaccinated, play in

Your puppy's coat may not need grooming, but he should get used to the routine.

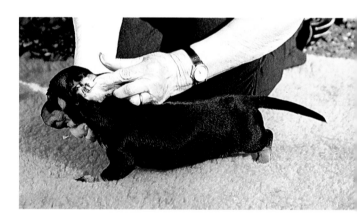

Accustom your puppy to having his ears examined.

Remember to keep a check on the mouth and teeth, particularly when your puppy is teething.

the garden will be all that is required. Work on some lead-training during this time to prepare the puppy for the time when he can be taken into the big outside world (page 43).

Up to the age of about six months, a couple of 10-minute walks a day is adequate, gradually increasing the length of the walks as the puppy grows. Around 14 months of age, the skeleton will have stopped growing, and your Dachshund can enjoy longer, more challenging walks.

Puppies need to be exposed to a wide variety of different situations so that they learn to be calm and well behaved.

Some experiences will have to wait until the puppy has had his vaccinations, but there are lots of things that you can organise while the puppy is still restricted to your home and garden (see below). Frequent visitors are a good start – the more contact the puppy has with people, the better.

If your puppy has been home-reared at the breeder's, he should already be familiar with household equipment such as vacuum cleaners, washing machines, and the television, which is a great advantage.

SOCIALISATION

Socialisation is the exposure of the puppy to different life experiences. If this happens while he is young, your Dachshund will grow up to be confident in all situations that he will encounter. A puppy isolated from the world will grow up to be nervous or aggressive, and it will be very difficult for him to overcome his fears.

Organising a puppy socialisation programme is quite simple, and is well worth the effort in the long term. Write down all the things that the puppy should be introduced to, and cross them off your list as you achieve them.

Pre-vaccination Socialisation

- Meet children of different age groups (see page 31)
- Meet elderly people
- Meet men and women of different ethnic backgrounds
- Play with balloons
- Exposure to people riding bicycles in your garden, rollerblading, or skateboarding
- Meet people wearing motorcycle helmets, hats etc.
- See people listening to personal stereos
- Meet people wearing sunglasses or carrying umbrellas

- Make short car trips (not only to introduce him to the outside world from the safety of the car, but also to accustom him to car travel).

Post-vaccination Socalisation
- Walk underneath a ladder
- Walk near traffic
- Travel on a bus, metro (subway), or train
- Visit a groomer
- Meet livestock if possible (sheep, cows, poultry). Always keep the puppy on the lead, and tell him "No" firmly if he becomes overexcited.
- Walk over bridges
- Walk on different surfaces, such as gravel, concrete, cobbles.

If your puppy shows any fear, give lots of reassurance and encourage him to sniff and investigate what is scaring him, so he realises it doesn't pose a threat. Often, puppies fearlessly sail through their early months, and then develop a phobic phase around nine months when they can become skittish and jumpy about the most innocuous things. Don't overreact when he exhibits fear, or you may make things worse. Be calm and confident, and he will regain his confidence (see Chapter Four).

PUPPY PARTIES
When you take your puppy to the vet for his initial check-up and vaccinations, ask about training classes and also ask if the practice runs puppy parties. These are doggie playschools or kindergartens, which are a useful preparation for the more formal training class that starts when the puppy is four to six months old, and they are an excellent way of getting the puppy used to other dogs and people from an early age.

TRAINING

Dachshunds are very independent dogs, and are renowned for having an obstinate streak, so your pup must learn, from the very start, that you are the pack leader. Training your dog is one way of earning his respect – and having an obedient dog will save you many blushes, and a lot of hassle, in the future.

The basic principle of successfully training your Dachshund is to keep training sessions short and fun, and to reward him whenever he successfully completes a task. If he does not do as you wish, be patient and try again.

HOUSE-TRAINING
Hopefully, the breeder will have started the puppy's house-training for you. If not, don't panic – house-training is very simple, provided you stick to a rigid routine.
- Decide beforehand on a toilet spot in the garden, somewhere the puppy will always be taken to relieve himself.
- Take your puppy outside to this spot frequently throughout the day. For the first few weeks, while the puppy has little control over his bladder, it is advisable to take him outside every two hours, in addition to the following times:

Establish a routine of taking your puppy out at regular intervals.

- Before settling for the night
- As soon as he wakes in the morning
- Before and after any naps throughout the day
- Before and after any periods of excitement (meeting visitors, play sessions)
- After a meal.

For the first few weeks, the house-training programme will be immensely successful, but don't fall into the trap of becoming complacent and thinking the puppy does not need such frequent attention – he does! You will have to do the puppy's thinking for him for many months to come, and any lapse on your part is likely to result in accidents recurring.

Routine

- Take the puppy to the allocated spot, and wait. Be patient. He will probably relieve himself eventually, but may need a little time to sniff around the garden first.

- When he performs, use a command word, such as "Hurry up" or "Be clean", so he learns to associate these words with the action. Eventually, you will be able to prompt him to relive himself by using these commands.
- Once the puppy has finished, praise him handsomely and give him a treat, so he knows he has done something good.
- Once you have cleaned up after him, enjoy some time in the garden together before returning indoors (otherwise, the pup may deliberately prolong 'going' in order to buy extra time in the fun outdoors).

Accidents

The best way to deal with mishaps is to prevent them. Once your puppy has an accident somewhere, he sets himself a precedent and may seek out the same spot next time he needs to relieve himself.

If your Dachshund has an accident, clean it up

CAUGHT IN THE ACT

If you catch him in the act, calmly distract him by calling his name in an excited way, and take him outside to his designated toilet spot so he can resume his business.

with a special cleaner (available from pet stores or from your vet) to remove all hint of the smell (ordinary ammonia-based cleaners actually smell like urine to a puppy!).

Do not be angry with the puppy if he has an accident. Shouting at him will make him fearful of you (he won't have a clue why you are yelling – after all, he's only answering a call of nature).

It may also have the added disadvantage of making him become more secretive about where he relieves himself in future. He may think you are scolding him for relieving himself, rather than because he has gone in the wrong place. As a result, he may avoid relieving himself in front of you, and may prefer to do it secretly (for example, behind the sofa) instead.

Remember – if your puppy has an accident, he is blameless. It is all your fault! Make sure you take him out more frequently to make sure it doesn't happen again.

NAME GAME

Try to choose a name for your puppy as soon as you can. Most breeders name the pups, and, if you like the name given to your Dachshund, stick with it. If not, choose another – your puppy will be young enough to adapt. Keep the name short, so it is easy for the pup to learn, and for you to say.

Familiarise the puppy with his name from the first day, and tell all your friends and family what the name is, so it is used by everyone he meets.

Say the name whenever you pet the puppy, when you give him a treat, or feed him a meal, so that he associates it with good things. With constant reinforcement, the puppy will soon learn what he is called.

COLLARED!

The first training sessions should focus on getting your Dachshund puppy used to wearing a collar. Use a light, soft collar, so that he will hardly notice what he is wearing. Put it on him, initially keeping it loose. Always supervise him when he is wearing a loose collar, though, as it could get caught on something.

Give him a delicious treat so he associates the collar with an enjoyable experience. He should concentrate on the treats you are holding, distracting his attention away from the collar. The more he wears the collar, the less unfamiliar

Use a soft, lightweight collar for early training sessions.

Use a treat to encourage your puppy to move forward on the lead.

CLICKER TRAINING

A clicker (available from most pet stores) is a small plastic box that fits snugly in the palm of the hand. It makes a distinct 'click' when pressed down with the thumb.

Clicker training is a popular method of training, which is very effective and simple to use. The basic principle is that the handler makes a click at the exact moment that the dog performs a desirable action. The click is then followed with lavish praise and a tasty treat. The Dachshund quickly learns to associate the click as a reward, and, eventually, the treats can be phased out.

Why not try some of the basic exercises in this chapter, using a clicker instead of the traditional treat-only reward?

it will seem. Put it on for short periods, many times throughout the day, gradually increasing the length of time it is left on.

When the puppy is used to wearing the collar, it should be tightened to its correct position, where you can comfortably fit two fingers underneath it. Remember to check the collar regularly – it will need adjusting as your Dachshund grows.

LEAD-TRAINING

Before your puppy has had all his vaccinations, you can start introducing him to the lead, in preparation for walks in public areas.

Once your pup is familiar with wearing a collar, attach a light lead and ask a member of the family to play with him. Follow the puppy around, holding the lead, but do not exert any pressure on it. This should prevent the bunny-hopping that can occur, where the puppy panics and jumps around to escape his 'shackles'.

Young puppies – usually under 16 weeks –

love following their owners around the house, so use this to your advantage while you still can! Attach the loose, light lead and walk around the house, tapping the side of your leg and calling him. Hold a favourite toy, if necessary, to encourage him to follow you. Praise him when he walks beside you.

Work on this exercise for short periods throughout the day, with the puppy on your left side. Hold the lead in your right hand, so it trails across your body, and hold any slack with your left hand, together with a treat or a toy to keep your puppy focused. Walk around the garden, around the house, and, when your Dachshund has had his vaccinations, practise in the park where there are other distractions.

If your puppy pulls ahead on the lead, do not yank him back – this will only encourage him to pull even more. Instead, just stop, call him to you, and start again. The puppy will soon realise that he doesn't get anywhere if he pulls.

When the puppy is walking beside you consistently well, his head close to your left leg (neither forging ahead nor lagging behind), then add a command word, such as "Heel", so the puppy learns to associate the correct position with the word.

SIT

The Sit is one of the most useful commands you can teach your Dachshund. If a puppy is chasing your cat, he can be stopped at once with "Sit". If he is about to run out of an open garden gate, "Sit" could avert a possible disaster. Or, if your puppy is under your feet in the kitchen, a "Sit" could settle him instantly.

If a treat is held above his head, your puppy will go into the Sit as he tries to reach for it.

- Kneel on the floor beside your Dachshund puppy.
- Show him that you are holding a treat. When he shows interest in it, and attempts to take it, move your hand above his head.
- When he stretches up to take it, move your hand further back a little (above his neck).
- To reach the treat in this position, the puppy will have to sit; he will not be able to achieve the height needed by standing.
- He may try to jump up to get it, but be patient and keep practising. Eventually he will sit.
- Just as he lowers his rear end to the floor, say "Sit" and give him the treat. Then enjoy some time out from the exercise for a couple of minutes.

Whenever your puppy sits of his own accord – wherever he is – say "Sit", praise him, and maybe give him a small treat. He'll probably think you've gone mad for being so excited about him sitting, but it will help to reinforce in his mind the association between the word "Sit" and the action.

DOWN

The Down command is taught using the same motivational method – luring the Dachshund into position with a treat, and rewarding his actions.

- Hold a treat in your hand, and lure the puppy into the Sit position (above).
- Instead of giving the puppy the treat, move your hand down to just in front of the puppy's paws.

Start with your puppy in the Sit.

*Lower the treat, and your puppy will follow it,
going into the Down position.*

- The puppy may break his Sit, stooping down to get the treat, but do not let him have it.
- Eventually, he will figure out that he can reach the treat only by lying down. As soon as he does this, say "Down", and give him the treat, along with lots of praise.
- Now the puppy has understood what is required, he will be quicker next time. With practice, he will eventually go down instantly on command, and you will no longer need to lure him. As with all training, treats can be phased out with time, so that you will only give them occasionally.

COME

Getting your Dachshund to come when called (recall) is an important lesson that you should start to teach your puppy from the first days that you bring him home.

You will find that your young Dachshund enjoys following you around the house (Dachshunds hate to think they might be missing out on something). Exploit your puppy's desire to be with you by teaching him the basics of recall before he becomes more independent.

- Ask a friend or family member to restrain the puppy gently, a couple of feet away from you.
- Kneel on the floor, then open your arms wide, call your Dachshund to you in an excited, jolly way, and ask him to "Come".
- The friend should let go as soon as you call the pup's name.
- When the puppy comes to you, give him a treat and a cuddle, and praise him.
- If the puppy is reluctant to come to you (which is rare), show him a treat or a favourite squeaky toy, to entice him to you.
- Practise a little every day, gradually increasing the distance between you and the puppy, and always making sure that you reward the pup.
- When your Dachshund will reliably come to you wherever you are in the same room, start to test his recall by your being out of sight. Hide in the kitchen and call him to you.
- Then take your practice sessions outside. Be warned: it is harder to maintain a puppy's concentration when there are distractions around, so his outdoor training might not be

Build up a good response to the "Come" command.

Work at the Stay, so that your puppy remains in position until you give the release command.

as successful as your indoor sessions.

- Practise the sessions regularly and introduce more distractions as your dog's training progresses – for example, arrange for a friend to walk some distance away while you are calling your Dachsie to you. This will all be excellent preparation for when you take your Dachshund into public parks, where there will be new sights, sounds and smells that will tempt him away from you.

- Never let your Dachshund off the lead in a public place unless you can fully trust his recall. Even if he is fully trustworthy, practise his recall throughout your regular walks. Call him to you every now and then during his exercise sessions, give him a treat if he complies, and then send him off again to enjoy himself.

STAY

Dachshund puppies rarely sit still for a second, so the Stay will pose quite a challenge! Doing nothing – which is all the Stay exercise is, in essence – is boring for a puppy, so it's your job to make it fun.

- Stand in front of your Dachshund, and put him into the Down position (above). Down-stays are the best starting place, as the dog is more likely to stay in position.

- When the dog is lying down, say "Stay" in a firm voice (so that you have his attention, but he is not encouraged to come to you). You can also hold your arm out in front of you, with the palm facing the dog, to reinforce that you do not want him to move.

- Wait five seconds and then give him the treat.

- Next, put him into the Down, take a step

back, and repeat.

- With short but frequent practice, very gradually increase the distance between you and the puppy, as well as the length of the Stay.

- Make sure that you always return to the dog, to give him a treat (if he comes to you for the treat, you are actually rewarding him for not staying).

- If the puppy ever looks as if he is about to break the Stay, say "No" firmly. If he moves anyway, don't be angry with him (it will just make him more insecure – and therefore less likely to Stay). Just start again.

THE SKY'S THE LIMIT

These are the basics for having a well-mannered dog. You can expand on your Dachshund's training quite easily, using reward-based training. For example, you can teach your puppy to find his lead and bring it to you. Simply give him his lead to hold and say "Lead". Then saying "Give", gently take the lead from him and give him a really tasty treat.

Then show him the lead, and put it on the floor a short distance from him. Say "Lead" in an excited way, and encourage him to get it. Puppies play with anything, so he won't need much encouragement to take it. As soon as he has it in his mouth, call him to you and say "Give".

Keep practising, placing the lead further away from the puppy, and eventually hiding it altogether. Dachshunds think with their noses, and your puppy will love finding his own lead. With practice, you can even move on to training your Dachshund to find your keys, or your wallet!

CHAPTER FOUR

THE ADOLESCENT DACHSHUND

When an angelic Dachshund puppy starts to have adult hormones coursing through his veins, the transformation into a 'terrible teenager' can be a traumatic time for owners! Some dogs are barely affected by adolescence, but many are, to a varying degree.

It is quite usual for a dog to test his owner's control at this time. For example, if the sofa is off-limits to your pet, a trying adolescent should be removed the moment he attempts to break the rules. Consistent leadership should get you through the next six months or so, and ensure that you and your Dachshund remain firm friends.

RECALL

Good recall (coming when called) is important for all breeds of dog, but, for the Dachshund, a typical hound, it is absolutely essential. When adolescence strikes, you may find that your Dachshund loses all memory of his earlier training, so practise the recall lessons from Chapter Three.

If, despite your revision of his early recall training, your Dachsie still refuses to come when called, invest in an extendible lead, which gives the dog a degree of freedom, but means you will remain in control. This will also ensure that the dog cannot run into a road, or disappear altogether. Here are some tips.

- Take your dog's food out on your walk – rattling his bowl will soon persuade him to return to you, and the food will act as his reward for being obedient.
- Call your Dachshund to you numerous times throughout his walk. If you only call him to you at the end of the walk, before taking him home, he will soon latch on to the connection, knowing that, if he complies, his walk comes to an end. Instead, call him to you every five minutes or so, give him a treat and then send him off again. Alternatively,

Rattling a food bowl will motivate your Dachsie to return to you.

teach him to fetch a ball, and bring it to you (see Chapter Six).

• Confusing your Dachshund is another good tip! The only reason your Dachshund runs off is that he knows you will be patiently waiting for him to return. If you become less dependable, however, he will stop taking you for granted. At any point on your dog's walk, suddenly change direction, hide, run away... do anything so that your Dachshund has to stay close by and watch you closely.

Be warned: when a Dachshund is following a really interesting smell, he becomes utterly focused on what he is doing – you could be setting off fireworks naked, and he wouldn't be aware of you. In such die-hard cases, you should seek the services of a professional trainer.

BARKING

The Dachshund is a noisy breed, bred to bark, alerting their handlers to their presence in the forest or down a rabbit hole. Dachshunds have retained this trait to the present day, and all self-respecting Dachsies think it is their duty to warn owners of any strange sounds, the approach of visitors, or the arrival of the post. Understandably, in a built-up urban area, the neighbours will not appreciate your dog's conscientiousness – and, after hours of continuous barking, you will probably lose your patience too.

It is useful, in some instances, to have a dog that barks. A warning bark when someone approaches the house is always appreciated, and, with the big-dog bark of a Dachshund, it can act as a deterrent to unwelcome visitors.

If your dog persists in barking, call him to you and give the command "Sit" or "Down".

However, any barking that you think is inappropriate should be eliminated.

- When your dog barks inappropriately, tell him "No" firmly. Do not shout or yell at him – you will only encourage him to continue barking.
- Call him to you, and command "Sit" or "Down", anything that will divert his attention and make him focus on you.
- Praise and reward him when he complies with your obedience commands.
- The instinct to bark is so strong in a Dachshund that you must remain firm, and patient. Don't give up, just because you think you are fighting a losing battle. Consistently quash inappropriate barking and it will become less habitual in the dog.

NERVOUSNESS

There is a tendency towards nervousness that runs right through the breed. This trait could arise from the work that Dachshunds were bred to do. If faced with a badger, or perhaps in the German forests, wild boar, the dog cannot afford to be too 'laid-back' or relaxed – he must be alert to every movement. Although, in the breed, there are examples of every type of temperament, from the 'couldn't care less' types right through to the almost pathologically nervous, it is fair to say that most Dachshunds exhibit nervousness at some stage in their life – particularly during adolescence when they lose their puppy boldness.

Prevention is better than cure. A comprehensive programme of socialisation (see Chapter Three) will show your puppy that the world is generally not a place to be feared. If your Dachshund becomes skittish, however, or if you have taken on an adolescent or adult rescued dog, you will have to take the time to re-socialise him.

When the dog becomes frightened, for whatever reason, do not panic or remove him from the object of his fears – this would serve only to reaffirm his belief that there really is something dangerous there, and that it has scared you too! Instead, remain calm, and talk to your dog quietly, reassuring him that he is safe. As with barking, some quick obedience exercises can also help, giving the dog something to concentrate on, and diverting his attention away from what he fears.

If your re-socialisation programme is not

If you are not planning to breed from your Dachshund, neutering is a sensible option.

progressing successfully, seek the advice of a qualified pet behaviour counsellor. Do not ignore the dog's problems, as he may develop more phobias that could stay with him for the rest of his life.

NEUTERING

Castration is a fairly simple operation, in which the testes are removed. Spaying is more complicated, involving the complete removal of the ovaries, but both procedures are now performed routinely. Although there is always a risk during surgery, neutering young, healthy animals is rarely problematic.

The age at which dogs are neutered varies according to each individual case, the owner's preferences, and the vet's own policy. It can range from as young as 12 weeks of age to 10 months and older.

Benefits

It is always best to spay or castrate your Dachshund unless you intend to become involved in showing or breeding – and if you are new to dogs and/or to the Dachshund, breeding is certainly not recommended. The main argument for neutering your Dachshund centres on the health benefits. A spayed female is likely to live longer, is unlikely to develop mammary tumours, and is free of the risk of developing pyometra, a life-threatening condition of the womb.

A castrated male can also enjoy a healthier life – free from prostate and testicular disorders. He is also less likely to be lost or killed through roaming after females in heat, and is unlikely to scent-mark and mount the furniture, or your guests.

On a more superficial level, a spayed female

does not present the owner with the inconvenience associated with her seasons, which occur roughly twice a year (see Chapter Two). Keeping a female away from males during her season can be very difficult, as she becomes a magnet for every canine Lothario in the neighbourhood.

With a spayed female, you can also rest easy at night, knowing your pet will not accidentally become pregnant and present you with a litter of puppies to care for and rehome, together with a hefty veterinary bill.

Spaying also prevents the problem of phantom pregnancies, when a Dachsie may start ripping up carpets to nest and stealing socks or soft toys to nurse, convinced she is pregnant when she is not.

Disadvantages

There are some risks when neutering an animal that you should be aware of when making your decision. In some cases, a character change can take place, with the Dachshund becoming more gentle and placid, and less 'plucky'. Most owners prefer a more cuddly, calm pet, so this 'disadvantage' can actually be seen as a benefit of neutering.

Some bitches develop a softer, more profuse coat after they are spayed. With pet dogs that are not shown, this is rarely seen as a matter for concern.

Weight gain is another common problem in neutered pets. However, if you are aware of this possible symptom, it can be averted by making sure the dog is exercised properly and not fed fatty or sugary treats, and by reducing the dog's daily food allocation (or switching to a light/lite brand).

Urinary incontinence in females is often regarded as a side effect of spaying. Some believe that the condition is the result of operating on very young animals, where the risk of damaging the bladder is increased. Others think it is related to the specific breed, and the shape of the pelvis and bladder. There is another school of thought that there is no increased risk of incontinence, and older unspayed females develop incontinence at the same rate as spayed animals. It is a contentious subject, and is one that you should discuss with your own vet.

The serious disadvantages of neutering are quite small statistically, and most people would agree that the benefits of neutering outweigh the disadvantages.

The spayed female will be easier to cope with, and she will also enjoy some health benefits.

CHAPTER FIVE

THE FAMILY DOG

The fun doesn't stop when your Dachshund leaves puppyhood. Now that all the hard work of raising a puppy is over with, you can sit back and look forward to years of companionship with your well-trained, well-socialised adult Dachshund.

Provided all his basic needs are catered for (feeding, exercise, and grooming), the Dachshund makes a great family dog, which loves and is loved by everyone in the house, both young and old. This is not a 'one-man' dog, crazy about only one member of the family; the Dachshund's loving, generous personality means he loves everyone to bits.

Ever adaptable, the Dachshund is a dog for all seasons and people – loving when you want a cuddle, workmanlike when you want a brisk walk, comical and clownish when you want to have fun playing with him. Whatever you want from a dog, the Dachshund pretty much fulfils every criterion.

HOME LIFE

To ensure that your Dachshund enjoys a fulfilling life, you should provide him with ample mental and physical stimulation. Take up a hobby together, such as Obedience, so you can spend quality time together. Chapter Six contains lots of ideas for different activities you can become involved in.

Just training your Dachshund to perform simple, fun tricks can keep his brain working, and this will be enjoyed by all the family, especially children. Here are a couple of ideas to get you started.

Shaking Hands

- Put your Dachshund in the Sit position, in front of you (see page 44).
- Show him a treat, touch one of his front paws gently, say "Shake", then give him the treat, together with lots of praise.
- Repeat, this time gently lifting his paw. Again, say "Shake" and reward handsomely.

Dachshunds love to please: A simple trick, like shaking hands, gives pleasure to both dog and owner.

- With practice, your Dachshund will automatically give his paw to you when you offer your hand – provided treats are on offer!
- Perform the exercise regularly, and your Dachshund will eventually 'shake hands' with anyone who says "Shake". It will make visitors feel extra welcome!

Roll Over

- Put your Dachshund in the Down position.
- Gently roll him on to his side, then on to his back, and finally on to his other side.
- While doing so, say "Roll", then give him a big cuddle, and a tasty treat.
- Make it fun. Don't be too serious or imposing, or your dog will be suspicious of you and won't want to co-operate.
- Practise little and often, so it becomes second nature to your dog, and always give him a reward when he rolls over, or he will lose interest.
- With time, you should be able to stop physically rolling the dog yourself; he will soon do it when he hears the command. As

soon as he does, praise and reward him handsomely, so he knows he has pleased you.

EXERCISE

Although the Dachshund (especially the Miniature) may look like a fragile little lapdog, nothing could be further from the truth. Originally bred as a tough, working hound, the Dachshund can hold his own in all weathers, and is much tougher than his cute good looks seem to suggest.

So don't skimp on your Dachshund's twice-daily walks, which should each last a minimum of 20 minutes, preferably longer. Remember: growing puppies do not need such a strenuous work-out (see Chapter Three).

Laziness breeds laziness, and, if a Dachshund gets out of the habit of regular walks, he can sometimes become reluctant to take any exercise at all (particularly in wet weather). A regular exercise routine, however, will keep your dog healthy in mind, body and spirit, and should stop him from becoming overweight (see page 59).

EXERCISING YOUR DACHSHUND

Despite his small size, the Dachshund is a true member of the hound family, and loves the opportunity to use his mind and his body.

ROVER RETURNS

Never let your Dachshund off the lead unless you are absolutely certain that he will come back when called. When they have their noses to the ground, sniffing out interesting scents, hounds can become utterly deaf to their owners' commands. Many disappear for hours – even days – and some may never return. Practise the recall exercises in Chapter Three in a safe, enclosed area (such as your garden). If you cannot trust your Dachsie to come to you when you ask him to, seek the advice of a professional trainer.

Taking the same walk twice a day, every day of the year, will be very boring for your Dachshund, and for you, so inject a little variety into his exercise regime. Take different routes on your walks; don't simply walk around the park and trot off home again – walk through woodland, on a beach, or across a field – so that you provide your Dachshund with new sights and smells to keep him alert.

You could also consider an alternative to a walk. Supervised swimming, for example, is also wonderful exercise.

When taking a walk, don't just plod around after your Dachshund; use the opportunity to get the very most out of your time together. Call him to you every now and again throughout the walk to refresh his recall skills (Chapter Three); throw toys for him to fetch; and hide from him, so he has to track you down. Use your imagination to make your walks fun and interesting, rather than a daily chore.

Never fail to clean up after your dog when he relieves himself in a public place. Inflicting the result of your laziness on other people is selfish and irresponsible, and gives all dogs and their owners a bad name. The most sensible option is to toilet your dog in the garden before leaving for a walk. You should still take a plastic bag to clean up after your Dachshund, just in case he is caught short later on.

FEEDING

The Dachshund is a dog that really loves his food. Occasionally, you will find a fussy eater, but, provided you haven't pampered your puppy, or given too many treats between meals,

TUNNEL VISION

If there is a rabbit hole within a three-mile (4.8 km) radius of where you walk your Dachshund, you can guarantee he will dive down it. Most come out eventually, once they have had their fun (and got thoroughly muddy in the process). However, some have a great knack of getting stuck down holes, and, sadly, some dogs disappear forever. Watch your Dachshund closely, so you know where he is at every moment, and perhaps attach a noisy bell to his collar so you can hear where he is. If your Dachshund is a serial tunnel dweller, you will just have to change the location of where you walk him off-lead.

Feed a well-balanced diet, and make sure your Dachshund never becomes obese.

feeding your adult dog should be plain sailing.

There is a variety of foods you can give, from home-prepared fresh meat and vegetables, to canned meat and biscuits, and complete dry foods. It is best to follow the advice of your Dachshund's breeder when choosing what to give your dog. Many people find the complete foods are the simplest to use, providing all the nutrients your Dachshund needs. They are easy to store, less messy than using fresh or canned meat, and simply require weighing out according to the dog's ideal weight.

If you wish to switch to a new brand or type of food, it should be done gradually so that your dog can become accustomed to the change (see Chapter Three).

Obesity

Obesity can be a big problem in Dachshunds, and the sight of overweight dogs waddling uncomfortably, with their bellies scraping against the ground, is not uncommon. It cannot be stressed enough that obesity should be avoided at all costs. It isn't simply a matter of

the dog looking terrible; his health will be adversely affected.

Obesity puts excess pressure on the heart, which has to work harder to accommodate the extra weight. Skeletal and joint problems can also result, with the spine and limb joints being put under strain from carrying too much fat.

Weigh your Dachshund regularly to make sure any weight gain is spotted early (it is surprising how difficult it is to spot when you see your dog every day).

Weigh yourself, and then weigh yourself holding your Dachshund, subtracting the first result from the second to ascertain your dog's weight.

If your dog is overweight, talk to your vet. Many surgeries have weight-loss clinics, with regular weigh-ins and lots of advice on losing the pounds.

Switching to a light ('lite') brand of food, cutting down on his ordinary food allocation, and giving fresh food (such as carrots) instead of sugary or fatty treats can all help to keep your Dachshund looking and feeling good.

HOME SWEET HOME

David Eley from Hampshire, UK, has always been a fan of big dogs, so when his wife, Linda, and two children, Daisy and Benty, suggested they take on a Miniature Dachshund, David wasn't enthusiastic... until he met Barton, a dog that has completely transformed his family life.

"I've had lots of dogs over the years, and seem to have a preference for large German breeds, such as Boxers and Dobermanns. I think every family should have a dog, but Linda didn't plan on becoming a dog owner, she claimed she wasn't a 'dog person'. I've never been drawn to small breeds, and really didn't relish the prospect of walking a tiny, coat-wearing dog in public. However, we live in

Barton: A little dog who made a big impact on his human family.

a small cottage, and, with two young children, we don't have the room for a large breed. Linda and the children kept seeing two Dachshunds when they went shopping, whom they were utterly enchanted by, and they persuaded me to consider a Miniature Smooth.

"After lots of research, and waiting for the right litter to turn up, we eventually took home Barton, an adorable red Mini Smooth-haired. Benty and Daisy (six and seven years respectively) were delighted. They had always wanted a dog – anything with legs, really! They have guinea pigs, but they don't really hold the same appeal as a puppy.

"Barton loves the guinea pigs – and their food. He sticks his nose in their cage and steals their lettuce. As a Dachshund, I'm sure it's in his blood to hunt small, furry creatures, but he just seems to love everything and everyone.

"Barton is wonderful with children. Linda takes him to pick up Daisy and Benty from school, where he meets all the pupils and runs around the playground with them. He was even spotted being kissed by the vicar at the end of school! Every night, we have a strict Barton-sharing routine. First, he goes to bed with Benty. In goes the hot-water bottle, followed by Barton, who dives under the covers. Twenty minutes later, when Daisy has finished reading, he goes to her room where he cuddles up for half an hour – his head on the pillow beside her.

"Every family should have a dog. It teaches children how to care and be responsible for an animal. Our children are not in charge of Barton (though they think they are), but dog ownership will teach them how to be considerate and kind towards other living creatures.

"Barton has been with us for only three months, but already it feels as if he has always been here. He has transformed our lives. It's extraordinary, really. There are a few miserable things going on in our lives at the moment (my parents are seriously ill), and Barton is a constant bright spot. No matter what's going on, he's there to make us smile."

GROOMING

All Dachshunds require a regular grooming routine. Obviously, the frequency and nature of that routine will vary depending on the coat type of your Dachshund.

Smooth-haired

This is the easiest coat type to maintain, requiring a weekly brushing and combing to get rid of any loose hairs, and to distribute the coat's natural oils through to the end of each hair. A rubdown with a hound glove will leave a lustrous shine to the coat. Check the feet, and trim any excess hair if necessary.

Wire-haired: The coat will need to be stripped twice a year.

Smooth-coated: A rubdown with a hound glove will bring out the sheen in the coat.

Wire-haired

Like the terrier breeds that have a harsh, non-shedding coat, the Wire-haired Dachshund needs to be stripped three or four times a year. Stripping involves the removal of the top coat, by plucking the individual hairs, which should already be loose. Some people use their forefinger and thumb; others use a stripping knife (where the hair is trapped between the blunt blade and the thumb, and then plucked). Be warned: stripping is a lengthy business, so set aside an entire day to do the job properly, or arrange for a professional groomer to do all the hard work for you! Make sure, however, that the groomer will strip the coat for you, rather than simply clip it (which will ruin the wiry texture, making it much softer, and lighter in colour).

The coat should be stripped in the spring and autumn, in preparation for hot and cold weather respectively. It is a fallacy that the coat should be kept long for the winter. It is not the length of

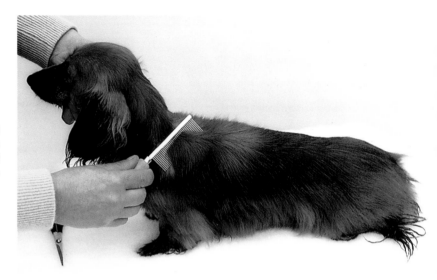

Long-haired. Thorough brushing and combing is needed to keep the coat tangle-free.

the coat, but the thickness of it, that is important in keeping a dog warm. Stripping the coat in autumn will give it plenty of time to thicken up with new hair for winter.

The best way to learn how to strip the coat is to watch an experienced breeder or groomer at work, but here are a few tips.

- Test a small patch of coat to check whether the coat is ready to be stripped. If the hair comes out easily when pulled, the time is right. If it is resistant in any way, do not progress. To do so will cause pain to your dog.
- Always strip in the same direction as the coat grows.
- Start at the head and work your way down the body.
- Leave the eyebrows and beard bushy.
- Use a pair of scissors to trim any hair around the feet, end of the tail, and ends of the ears to produce clean, neat edges.
- Cut away the hair underneath the feet, in

between the pads and toes. This will stop it from collecting mud, which can cause sores.
- Finish off with a final comb through and a rubdown with a hound glove.
- Trim around the feet to create a neat line, and cut any excess hair between the pads.

In between these strips, the coat should be brushed through daily with a bristle brush. It's a quick job that should take no more than a couple of minutes.

Long-haired

The Long-haired coat needs grooming at least three times a week to prevent mats and tangles from forming. A bristle brush should be used on most of the body, with a comb for the parts where the hair is not so dense (such as on the ears and feet). Tangles are quick to form under the armpits, elbows, stomach, and behind the ears, so do not neglect these areas when grooming.

After a grooming session, scissors can be used to tidy up the dog every now and again. The hair between the pads can be cut back, and a neat line can be achieved by carefully snipping excess hair around the feet.

BATHING

It is only necessary to bath your Dachshund when he really needs it – if he's rolled in something nasty, or has dived down a swampy, muddy hole, for example. In most cases, a muddy dog can be dried and brushed thoroughly, to make the coat come up as good as new.

Most dogs need a bath only once or twice a year. To bath the dog any more frequently can ruin the coat, softening it in the case of the Wire, and drying it out in the case of the Smooth- and Long-haired.

- Stand your Dachshund in the bath tub or shower cubicle, on a non-slip mat.
- Wet his coat thoroughly with warm water, reassuring him all the time. If necessary, ask a friend to restrain the dog gently but firmly, so he doesn't jump around in the bath or try to climb out.
- Apply a little mild shampoo to the coat, and massage into the coat until it is all lathered, right down to the skin.
- Shampoo around the ears, but shield the dog's eyes from any soapy water. If you use a mild dog shampoo, it shouldn't hurt if a little gets in his eyes, but do rinse the eyes thoroughly if this occurs.
- Rinse the coat thoroughly.

- Tickle just inside the dog's ears to encourage him to shake the excess water from the coat, while he is still standing in the bath or shower cubicle.
- Lift him out and dry the coat. With Smooth-hairs and Wire-hairs, you can rub the coat briskly with a towel. With Long-hairs, it is best to squeeze the moisture out, by pressing with a towel.
- Smooth- and Wire-haired Dachshunds can be left to dry naturally in a warm room. Long-haired dogs will need their coats to be blow-dried. Because the coat should lie close to the body in this Dachshund variety, some people put the dog's body into a nylon stocking or cover it with a towel while drying the coat, to keep it flat.
- If you show your dog (of whatever coat type), bath him at least a week beforehand, so the coat has time to settle before the dog is exhibited.

GENERAL CHECKS

A regular grooming session also provides an opportunity for you to check over your dog. Feel him all over, and ask yourself the following questions:

- Are there any unusual lumps and bumps?
- Are there any tender areas that cause your dog pain?
- Are there any cuts or scratches?
- Is the dog overweight or underweight?
- Is his bottom clean?
- Is there evidence of fleas or other parasites in the coat?

Ears

Now, turn your attention to your Dachshund's pendulous ears. Because the ears are not erect and so do not get very much air circulating around them, they are more prone to infections, and mites just love the warm, dark crevices of a Dachsie's ears. Look out for any of the following:

• Dirty ears
• Smelly ears
• Red, sore, or hot ears.

If your dog keeps scratching at his ears, or shaking his head, or shows any of the above signs, seek veterinary advice. If the ears are dirty but your dog is not showing any symptoms of mites or infections, you can attend to them by using a special cleaner, which you can buy from your vet or pet store. In most cases, the nozzle should be inserted into the ear, and the liquid squeezed into the opening of the ear canal.

Check the ears to make sure they are clean and fresh-smelling.

When the liquid is applied, massage the outside of your dog's ears – most dogs appreciate the soothing sensation. Then your Dachshund will shake his head, removing the liquid (and the loosened dirt) from his ears. Because it can be quite a messy job, you might want to do it outside, to save your wallpaper and carpets!

Regularly check the hair growth in your dog's ears. Wire-haired Dachshunds will need some of the hair removed from inside the ear. Pluck it out firmly but gently in the same way you would strip the coat.

After each walk, check your dog's ears to make sure he hasn't picked up any grass seeds and so on. This can be a particular problem for the Dachshund, who invariably walks with his head down, investigating everything he encounters.

Teeth

Check your Dachshund's mouth, teeth, and gums every week. If your dog has very bad breath, he will probably need to have a veterinary dental procedure (for which sedation is usually required), to have his teeth scaled properly

To prevent your dog's teeth from deteriorating to this point, he will need to have his teeth brushed at least once a week. Use a long-handled, firm-textured toothbrush, and apply a little canine toothpaste (meaty-flavoured ones are available from pet stores). Brush every tooth carefully, away from the gums, reassuring your dog as you do so. If you have accustomed your puppy to this procedure from an early age,

Regular tooth-brushing will prevent the accumulation of tartar.

he will not struggle – he will be too busy trying to lick the tasty toothpaste.

Teach an adult dog to enjoy the process, by gently opening his mouth, then giving him a treat. Progress to touching his gums, then rubbing toothpaste on to his teeth, using your finger, or a rubber fingerbrush that fits over your forefinger. After each session, give him a treat, so he learns to associate having his teeth and mouth touched with an enjoyable experience.

Nails

A well-exercised dog, walked on a variety of hard and soft surfaces, should have no need for his nails to be trimmed. However, if you have an older dog, who is exercising less, you will need to check his nails regularly. If they are long, use guillotine-type nail clippers to trim the ends, until they are the correct length. Do not chop off a lot in one go, as you may accidentally cut into the dark central part of the nail, which is the quick – the nerves and blood supply to the nail. This will be very painful for the dog, and may also cause a nail infection, too. If you are

uncertain about the procedure, it is wise to ask your vet or groomer to do it for you, and to observe what is done.

Do check your Dachshund's dewclaws, if they haven't been removed at birth. The dewclaw is positioned further up the foot, and will not wear down naturally. If it becomes too long, it will curl around, and start digging into the dog's leg, so check the dewclaws regularly, and trim if required.

Feet

You will also need to check your dog's feet, check between the toes and pads for any clumps of dried mud (which can lead to sores), or for any foreign bodies (such as grass seeds) that may be lodged there. The Long-haired

Trim the tips of the nails with guillotine-type nail clippers.

The owner of two adult Dachshunds, Oscar and Sparky, Lisa Watson from Wiltshire, England, had never considered taking on a rescued dog. Following the unexpected death of Oscar, however, Lisa was forced to consider taking on a new adult dog as company for the grief-stricken Sparky.

"Oscar, a Mini Wire, was our first Dachshund," explains Lisa. "When he was 11 years old, we bought a Mini Smooth puppy named Sparky. They adored each other, and were a great team. Sadly, Oscar died a year later. We were all distraught at losing him – my husband Mark and the children, David (then aged nine) and Caroline (then six) but Sparky took it especially badly. He pined terribly for Oscar, and wouldn't eat. He was going downhill fast.

"I contacted a well-known breeder for advice, who was also involved in the breed rescue organisation, and she suggested I get a new companion for Sparky: a small, year-old Standard Long, called Pebbles, who had not long been in a rescue organisation. I was a little uncertain about taking on another dog, as Oscar had died just four days previously, but, for Sparky's sake, we all went to meet Pebbles.

PAST PAIN

"Pebbles had a rather chequered history. She had lived in an apartment, with her disabled owners and five other dogs. She had been allowed to relieve herself in the house, as I don't think it was easy for the owners to take her out very much. She was poorly socialised, and was scared of everything, particularly things with wheels, such as bicycles, skateboards, and wheelchairs.

"We spent an hour with Pebbles, and we all

Pebbles: A much-needed companion for Sparky.

fell in love with her. She was very timid at first, but after a while she calmed down a bit. She growled at the children on the first meeting, which concerned me, but I think it was simply because she hadn't experienced children before – she didn't know how to behave around them.

"When we took Pebbles home, we were all very careful around her, making sure we didn't make any loud, sudden movements or noises, and generally building up her confidence and trust. The children were told not to lie down on the floor with their faces close to Pebbles's face, as we weren't sure how she would react. Her tail was also off-limits, as she was quite sensitive about people touching it.

"Pebbles's discipline also had to be handled sensitively. If we raised our voices, she would hide under the furniture for a couple of hours. We had to show her that if she did something wrong, we would tell her off firmly, but that we wouldn't smack or hurt her. Within a very short time, we gained Pebbles's trust.

"Training her to be clean in the house was quite simple. It was like having a puppy again, having to take her out at frequent intervals throughout the day.

PUPPY AT HEART

"Pebbles is a very small Standard Dachshund, and looks rather like a puppy. She now behaves like one, too. I don't think she had been given the opportunity to be a real puppy when she was younger, but she more than made up for this once she settled in with us! She played with the children for hours, and also with Sparky, who regained his zest for life.

"A year later, Sparky and Pebbles are inseparable; they play, groom, and curl up asleep together, and have become the very best of friends. We couldn't be happier with the way things have turned out."

It is a good idea to check your Dachshund's feet after walks.

Dachshund is particularly prone to bringing home half of his walk in his coat and feet.

Walking on sand or in salty water can dry out the pads and cause them to crack. Wash the feet thoroughly if they have been in contact with salt, then dry them, and apply a little petroleum jelly.

After a walk in snow or ice, dry the feet thoroughly, as the hair around the feet can freeze and cause sores.

Seek veterinary advice if your Dachshund has sustained any serious injuries (such as stepping on glass), or if you are at all concerned about his wellbeing.

RESCUED DACHSHUNDS

If you don't have the time or inclination to take on a demanding Dachshund puppy, why not consider a rescued dog? An adult rescued

Dachshund will still need lots of time and patience for trust to be built between you, but an older dog will probably be already house-trained. He will usually sleep undisturbed through the night, and his feeding regime will be less demanding.

The number of Dachshunds that need rehoming is relatively small. Those that are up for adoption are usually in rescue through no fault of their own – often as a result of a marriage break-up or the death of an owner. Very few are put into a shelter because of behavioural problems.

If you are thinking of taking on a rescued Dachshund, contact a breed rescue organisation which can often give more specialised advice than an all-breed organisation. Your national breed club will have details of a reputable rescue group that you can contact.

VETERAN CARE

A relationship with an oldie can be an extra-special one. There is an intimacy between pet and owner, developed through years of interaction and closeness, almost to the point where you can second-guess each other's actions. Older dogs often crave their creature comforts (such as a soft, warm spot to sleep on), and generally like to snooze more – so that means more cuddles for you!

The Dachshund is a lively, fun breed that remains young at heart throughout his life. Compared to some other breeds, he is also long-lived, often surviving into his mid- or late-teens.

Every dog is an individual, and some may appear old at 10, while other dogs of the same age may still be as sprightly and bouncy as the day they were brought to their new home. There are no hard-and-fast rules to looking after an older dog. Just assess your dog's evolving needs and act accordingly. Here are a few pointers.

Deafness

Like all breeds, older Dachshunds can become a little deaf. When the dog is young, incorporate hand signals into your general training, which will come in very useful if the dog loses his hearing later in life. Also be aware that a dog which is hard of hearing will not hear you approach. Be particularly gentle when waking an older dog, who could otherwise jump out of his skin!

Exercise

Let your dog dictate his own exercise requirements. Don't force a very old Dachshund to take a walk. If he isn't keen, and would rather enjoy a nap, let him, and try to exercise him later.

Three or four short, gentle strolls a day are preferable to two long hikes, and help to keep your oldie mentally alert, without putting his body under undue strain.

Warmth

Dachshunds, like all other dogs, can suffer from arthritis, a condition often exacerbated by the damp and cold. After a walk, make sure you dry your dog, and ensure his bed is in a warm, draught-free area.

Dachshunds generally live to a ripe old age. This is Ch. Minimead Miss Marple, aged 13 years.

Grooming

Your dog's coat may become thinner and more dull-looking (especially in spayed bitches). Don't neglect regular grooming, particularly as it provides the opportunity to check your Dachshund to ensure he is fit and healthy.

Your dog's nails may need trimming if he is receiving less exercise and is not, therefore, wearing them down naturally (see page 65).

Anaesthesia is more risky in older dogs, so try to avoid the need for a veterinary dental procedure by regularly cleaning your pet's teeth.

Diet

If your oldie is taking less exercise, his energy requirements will also be less. Consider switching to a 'light' or 'senior' variety of complete food. If you feed meat and biscuits, perhaps give more vegetables than meat.

On no account allow your Dachshund to pile on the pounds. Arthritic conditions are exacerbated by excess weight, and you will be putting undue pressure on your dog's heart and back (see page 59).

Some breeders recommend adding a little fish oil to a veteran's diet to help his mobility and coat condition. Ask your vet for details.

Character

How your dog's character develops with old age very much depends on the individual. If your Dachshund has always been bad-tempered around other dogs, he may become even less tolerant of them. If he is a 'clingy' dog, this aspect of his personality could also be accentuated.

If your dog behaves totally uncharacteristically, you should seek veterinary advice – for example,

MOBILITY AIDS

Some Dachshunds, particularly older ones, can develop very weak hindlegs, often through arthritis. In dogs who have an otherwise healthy, fulfilling life, this disability can be overcome by way of a sling.

A sling is a simple aid, which you can make from a strong, soft piece of material which is placed under the dog's tummy, by his hindlegs. When your Dachshund needs to go outside, or needs a walk, you can hold the material up, to support his rear end, while the dog walks normally on his front legs.

Alternatively, there are dog 'carts' or 'trolleys' on the market. These are two-wheeled contraptions in which the dog's rear end is secured. The dog can then move around simply using his front legs, with the rear end scooting behind.

If you would like more infomation, these carts are often advertised in the dog press, or perhaps your vet may have a contact for a local manufacturer.

if a usually good-tempered dog starts being aggressive, it could be because he is in pain.

LETTING GO

Euthanasia is a subject that all pet owners have to face at some point in their lives. Sadly, it is very rare for an elderly dog to die peacefully in his sleep, and there comes a time when the difficult decision to put your dog to sleep has to be made.

Veterinary medicine is improving all the time, and it is now possible to manage a whole host of conditions that were untreatable just a few years ago. Pain relief, too, can be used to good effect, ensuring that dogs enjoy happy, pain-free lives for longer.

However, medicine cannot keep a dog alive indefinitely, and there will come a time when your vet will tell you that all treatments have been exhausted, and there is nothing more that can be done for your Dachshund.

Such a moment is the very worst part of pet ownership, but is one for which you should be prepared. The moment you take on a puppy, you should remind yourself that you are this creature's guardian right through to the end of his life. You are responsible for his wellbeing, and that includes making sure he does not suffer unnecessarily. Hard though it is to say goodbye, euthanasia is the final act of love for your best friend.

Facing life without your pet can be extremely tough, and many people are surprised at how deeply depressed they feel afterwards – particularly owners who have never been through losing a pet before.

Talk to dog-owning friends, or specialist pet bereavement counsellors (your vet surgery should be able to point you in the right direction). There are also a number of helpful websites on the internet devoted to the subject – use a reliable search engine to search for pet-loss sites.

SAYING GOODBYE

Cancer had robbed Maggie Rowe of her husband, mother, and best friend, all within a few weeks of each other. When her Dachshund, Jenny, developed a lump in her cheek, Maggie was faced with the awful prospect of losing another loved one to the terrible disease.

"I never used to like Dachshunds; I thought they were ugly little creatures!" says Maggie, a photographer from Hertfordshire, England. "Until, that is, I was given one as a present. Within a week, I was besotted. That was 30 years ago, and I've had them ever since.

"For me, the decision to put an animal to sleep has never been a difficult one. I just do whatever is right for the dog. That's not to say that it doesn't hurt – it is terribly painful to lose a dog. They are members of the family, aren't they?

"The most awful times concerned Jenny, a Miniature Smooth. She was one of my favourite Dachshunds ever. She was very special – so full of life and kindness. She helped me through the deaths of my husband, mother and best friend, which all occurred within a short space of time. She gave me unconditional love

Jenny: Full of life and full of kindness.

and support when I needed it most. At the time, I remember thinking, 'Thank God for Jenny.'

"Within a few weeks, though, I noticed she had a bump in her cheek. I feared the worst. I took her to the vet, and the lump was removed and was found to be a malignant cancer. A friend of mine, who is a pathologist, told me that if the cancer came back, I should consider putting Jenny to sleep at once. Just a week later, Jenny's face had ballooned with another lump. It was a particularly virulent cancer, as my friend had suspected.

"I knew at once that I couldn't let Jenny suffer. A human would have had to face months of prolonged agony, but it wasn't fair to make Jenny suffer, when she could be put to sleep peacefully. It is real love to do that for your pet.

"You can't prepare for the loss you feel afterwards. It is as bad as losing a member of the family, but without the sympathy. I remember, with my first dog, someone saying to me, 'Well, you can buy another one!'. But it isn't that simple. You need time to grieve, just as you would for any other loved one. With time comes a gradual acceptance, and the pain slowly starts to ease."

CHAPTER SIX

BROADENING HORIZONS

Laziness is an accusation frequently levelled at the breed, and the Dachshund certainly enjoys lounging around, cuddling up with his family, but, equally, he would become a very bored little dog if he had no other stimulation in his life. Being a working breed, the Dachshund loves to have a job to do, and likes to be kept active, mentally and physically.

There are lots of different activities you and your Dachshund can enjoy together, to suit your personal preferences, the dog's age and level of fitness, and the time you can dedicate to the hobby. Read on to find something that suits you – and enjoy life with your Dachshund to the utmost.

CANINE GOOD CITIZEN

The 'Good Citizen' scheme is an excellent starting point for all dog owners who want to expand on their dogs' initial training and socialisation. The American Kennel Club has the Canine Good Citizen Program and the British Kennel Club endorses the Good Citizen Dog Scheme. Both programmes aim to produce a new generation of impeccably-behaved dogs that are sufficiently trained and socialised to cope in a number of different everday situations, such as:

• Being handled and groomed
• Responding to basic obedience commands
• Meeting another dog
• Walking on a loose lead in a controlled manner
• Walking confidently through a crowd of people
• Being approached and petted by a friendly stranger.

If you have trained and socialised your Dachshund from an early age, as suggested in Chapter Three, the tests shouldn't prove too much of a challenge, and can be another way of topping up your dog's social and training skills. There are many participating training clubs in most locations where you can enrol in Good Citizen classes to prepare your dog for the tests. To find out more information on the schemes, contact your national kennel club.

OBEDIENCE

If you have enjoyed your puppy's basic training (see Chapter Three), and would like to take it further, why not consider Competitive Obedience? The Dachshund is not a breed that is a natural in the sport, as Border Collies or German Shepherd Dogs are, but some people have done quite well with their Dachshunds, and have had fun training their dogs along the way.

If you are fiercely competitive, it's best to consider another breed; but if you are of the mind that it is the competing, not the winning, that is important, you and your dog could get a lot of enjoyment from the sport.

The first thing to do is to join an Obedience training club (your national breed club or kennel club will have details). To give you a taste of some of the exercises involved, try some of the following.

HEELWORK

Your puppy should already be walking well on the lead (see Chapter Three). For Competition Heelwork, however, the dog is expected to be much closer to the handler, his shoulder level with the owner's left leg, and he should walk

The Dachshund must focus his attention on the handler, and maintain a close heelwork position.

well both on and off the lead. It is not easy to teach a Dachshund to heel correctly, but regular, short, fun practice, a little a couple of times a day, will aid your progress. If your Dachshund believes heelwork is an enjoyable game, he will prove a more willing pupil.

- Place your Dachshund in the Sit beside your left leg.
- Hold the lead in your right hand, keeping your left hand free to give hand signals to the dog.

- Call your dog's name, so that he looks at you (but his body should remain facing forward).
- Take a couple of steps forward, starting with your left leg, and encourage the dog to walk with you (for example, use your left hand to tap your left leg).
- Command "Heel" when the dog walks in the correct position, then praise enthusiastically.
- Stop walking, and ask the dog to "Sit" next to you, in the original position you started with. From the beginning, encourage the dog to sit facing forward; a Dachshund that gets into the habit of sitting crooked is difficult to correct at a later stage.
- Praise the dog for doing well, and give a treat as a reward. It is important to maintain the dog's interest in training, and introducing food will certainly keep a Dachshund focused!
- Practise a few more times, and finish the session with a game, so that your Dachshund does not become bored and resent his training sessions.
- With subsequent sessions, reward only the very best heelwork positions, until the dog's performance is consistently good.
- Next, you can introduce more variety. Practise heeling at a slow pace, fast pace, and a mixture of paces.
- When the dog can heel well at different speeds, start to introduce turns.

Instead of walking in a straight line, veer to the left slightly, gradually introducing more pronounced turns, until, eventually, the dog will stick close to you even when you do a complete about-turn.

THE RETRIEVE

The Dachshund is not a natural retriever. However, with the right motivational training, most Dachshunds can be taught to retrieve a dumb-bell, your car keys, or a toy. As before, keep training sessions short and fun, and use lots of rewards to maintain your Dachshund's interest.

You can nurture the retrieve instinct by encouraging your Dachshund to hold balls or toys in his mouth while he is still a puppy. Call him to you while he has an item in his mouth, and give plenty of praise when he comes to you. Take the item from his mouth, and give him a treat. Then give the toy straight back to him, so that he doesn't resent giving it to you.

The Hold

You should get your Dachshund used to holding hard items in his mouth; the dumb-bell that is retrieved in Obedience is made of hard plastic or wood. Buy a small dumb-bell, one that is about $3/4$ of an inch thick (2 cms). If your Dachshund does not like the sensation of holding the dumb-bell, cover it with a towel or thick material at first, removing it once your Dachshund is happy to have it in his mouth.

- Kneel on the floor and sit your Dachshund in front of you.
- Gently open his mouth, place the dumb-bell over his lower jaw, and close his mouth.
- Say "Hold", and wait for just a second or two, still keeping the dog's mouth shut.
- Take the dumb-bell from him, saying "Give" as you do so.

TEACHING THE RETRIEVE

Left: The dog is commanded to "Wait" while the dumb-bell is thrown.

Above: The dog runs out and picks up the dumb-bell.

Right: The dog returns to the handler and presents the dumb-bell.

- Then praise him, give him a treat, a cuddle, then a game, so he feels very clever and special.
- Practise little and often, until your Dachsie will take the dumb-bell without help, and gradually extend the length of time he holds the dumb-bell.

Fetch

- Next, you want to start training your Dachshund to take the dumb-bell from different locations.
- Over the course of a few training sessions, start holding the dumb-bell lower down than usual. Work until you can place the dumb-bell on the ground, and your Dachsie is happy to pick it up without assistance.

- Then put the dumb-bell a little further away from the dog, so he has to walk to it, fetch it, then return to you, sit in front of you, and wait until the dumb-bell is taken from him.
- Don't forget to make a big fuss of your Dachshund when he has done well.
- Finally, put your Dachshund on an extendible lead, and place him in the Sit position on your left side.
- Throw the dumb-bell a little way in front of you both, keeping the lead short so that he can't chase after it.
- Tell him "Wait" firmly (see Chapter Three), then extend the lead and tell him to "Fetch". By now, it will be second nature to him to fetch the dumb-bell and to sit in front of you until it is taken from him.

WINNIE TAKES ALL

Winnie is an eight-year-old red Smooth Miniature Dachshund, who weighs just 9 lbs. Owned by Marivonne Rodriguez from Houston, Texas, USA, Winnie is an incredibly versatile dog, accomplished in many areas of training, including Obedience, Freestyle, Agility and Tracking.

"Winnie is the first dog in my 'adulthood', with me being the sole caretaker. I had dogs throughout my childhood, though, including a Lhasa Apso and a Pekingese. I have always favoured small dogs, and I prefer females.

"I actually considered a Pug at first, but I couldn't find a female pup. That's when I considered that a comical, cute little Dachshund might do the trick. I read about their often-clownish personalities, their loyalty for their owners, their excellent watchdog capabilities, plus their small size and smooth coat, and thought a Mini Smooth would be very practical budget-wise, as well as for my apartment lifestyle.

"Winnie is my heart and my soul; my 'dog who can do no wrong'. In her youth, though, Winnie was actually quite fearful of people and other dogs. She was very shy, very introverted, and even snapped at my first Obedience instructor (it was a fear-induced reaction). She underwent quite a bit of desensitization to try to fix this.

"Winnie is still pretty cautious and reserved around other dogs, but training has done wonders to 'cure' her people fears, and she is all sugar with everyone now. Her tongue will have to be indicted in the Licking Hall of Fame: she is one lean, mean, licking machine. She doesn't stop – she can lick you right down to the bone if you let her!

WINNIE TAKES ALL ▶

Winnie: Her motivation is food, food, food!

WINNIE TAKES ALL

BATTLE OF WILLS

"Training-wise, I describe Winnie as my 'Make me' dog. In the early stages of our training, 'Make me' seemed to be her motto. At that time, clicker training wasn't nearly as popular as it is now, and my instructor used more traditional compulsion methods, though we rewarded Winnie with food.

"Her eyes would say things like, 'And I should do this because...?', 'And this benefits me how?', or 'That's nice, but my plans are different from yours'. It was a battle of wills at first.

"Now, training Winnie is like driving a car in cruise control. I can sit back and she pretty much drives herself.

EARLY TRAINING

"I started Winnie's basic Obedience training when she was around six months old. After finishing that first eight-week class, we were hooked. My instructor said she noticed that Winnie may have the makings of a competition Obedience dog. And so on to competition Obedience training we went. We haven't stopped doing training of one kind or another since.

"My favourite Obedience exercise is heeling. However, if you only do the prescribed pattern as will be done in the ring, it can get pretty boring, pretty quickly.

"In order to spice things up for Winnie, I began teaching her twirls, 360-degree turns in place (on the spot), backing up from in front and from heel position. All with the purpose of keeping heeling interesting for her.

"We tend to use fast music for our Freestyle moves. While I enjoy listening to some of the softer, tear-jerker tunes that some folks in Freestyle like to use, Winnie might just fall asleep on me if I were to use that for our dancing! Something fast and fun is best for her.

"I am thinking of entering Winnie in some Freestyle competitions soon. As she gets older, she may be less able to do the jumping in Obedience or Agility, and so Freestyle might just be her cup of tea.

"Winnie's motivation is food, food, food, food! She is extremely food-motivated. She also loves playing fetch, so I bring this game into our training sessions.

"She can't do too much of any one thing – she loses enthusiasm very quickly – so our training sessions have to be short (a maximum of 30 minutes), with lots of different cookies, and balls for fetching.

AGAINST ALL ODDS...

"To be successful, you have to know how to train a Dachshund, and which methods to use. Traditional 'yank 'em and jerk 'em' methods do not work with the breed. So if that's the method someone wants to use with their dog, I wish them the best of luck. But if you make training worth a dog's while, if they see that there's something in it for them, they'll bend over backwards for you.

"Here, in the United States, you now see more and more Dachshunds in Obedience rings than you would have seen 10 or 15 years ago, and I attribute it to the change in training philosophies and methods that the Obedience community has adopted.

"If I had listened to all the people who said that, to do well in Obedience, you have to have a Border Collie, I wouldn't have gotten to where I have with Winnie.

"Her accomplishments are many – she was nationally ranked every year she was shown, she has her Utility Dog Obedience title, she has won the National Specialty in 1998, has multiple perfect heeling scores, and she has qualified to compete at a regional tournament... Now, you tell me Dachshunds are dumb!"

FREESTYLE

If you would like to jazz up your Obedience moves, Freestyle or Heelwork to Music is worth considering. Derived from traditional Obedience exercises, such as Heelwork, Freestyle involves 'dancing' to music with your dog. It is brilliant fun – great to watch, and even better to do, and dogs love it.

Marivonne Rodriguez (see Case History, page 77) has incorporated Freestyle into her general Competition Obedience training, in order to vary the exercises and to hold her Dachshund Winnie's interest. She uses a clicker for as much of her training as possible, giving a click at the exact time that Winnie performs correctly. She also uses cookies to lure Winnie at first, and toys as stress relief during and after sessions.

SPINS

"I taught the spins in place (on the spot) with the aid of a target stick. Winnie had been trained to touch the tip of a stick for her Obedience training, so, when shown that stick, she would follow it in order to try to touch it. I clicked when she followed it and then just directed the stick in the direction I wanted her to go. Pretty soon, I had her spinning in place, then I was able to make the stick smaller and smaller, until my index finger became the stick, and, hence, the signal for her to spin in place."

WEAVING

"Weaving between the legs, both in a figure of eight and in a straight line, is taught with food luring, clicking when the dog goes through the right leg in the correct direction. This is done with the handler being stationary, at first. As the dog becomes more proficient, the handler can start to take a step forward, then two steps and so on. until, eventually, the dog will be weaving gracefully through the legs as the handler walks briskly forward."

AGILITY

Agility is best described as a canine obstacle course. Dogs must complete the course as accurately and quickly as possible. Obstacles include hurdles, long jumps, tunnels/chutes (which Dachshunds particularly love), poles that the dog should weave through, a seesaw (teeter), an A-frame (steep A-shaped ramp), and a narrow, elevated plank or walkway.

The Dachshund is not a breed that first comes to mind when one considers Agility, but, in the United States, there are quite a few Dachshies that compete in the sport.

Because Agility is a physically demanding activity, puppies and growing dogs are not allowed to compete. This safety precaution is especially important in a breed such as the Dachshund, with his long back and short legs. In the United States, most of the Agility Dachshunds are Minis, or very small Standards. A full-sized Standard usually qualifies for a bigger hurdle height, which can be too much of a strain.

If you would like to learn more about training for Agility, ask your kennel club or breed club for details of your nearest club.

Like many Dachshund owners, Dan and Debby McNamara are committed to training their dogs to a high standard in a number of different disciplines, including Agility.

"We got our first dog, a red, Long-haired Miniature Dachshund named Oscar, in 1984," say Dan and Debby, from Franklin, Wisconsin. "He was so cute and friendly, we just had to bring him home. Four years later, we decided to get Oscar a companion and playmate, so we bought Barney (Barney Rubble of Forest Hill), a black-and-tan Miniature Long-hair. Our newest addition to the family is another Dachsie – a red sable Mini Long called Pete.

"We also have two Border Collies: Fred and Twister. When we got our first Collie, Fred, we knew we needed an activity to keep him busy, and became involved in Agility. After

Barney: Once his attention is focused, he is a great Agility enthusiast.

about a year of training Fred, we decided to try training Barney.

"Barney had been training in Obedience up to this point, but Agility seemed to be a more difficult event for a Dachshund, due to the physique. Dan decided to give it a try anyway, and, in 1992, Barney started training in Agility at the age of four-and-a-half.

"Training a Border Collie and a Dachshund are very different tasks. Collies have a natural drive to work – they want to work. They find it rewarding to perform a task for their master.

Dachshunds, on the other hand, need to be persuaded to perform certain tasks. In training, food has been a great motivator for Barney. As long as he knows he has a treat coming, he'll do almost anything!

OVERCOMING PROBLEMS

"Scent distractions can be a problem when working with the Dachshund. It is natural for a hound to sniff, but we worked on the 'Leave it!' command to stop Barney from sniffing at inappropriate times.

"Jump heights were another concern, and slowed Barney down considerably. It was very noticeable, after Barney turned eight years old, that 12-inch (30-cm) jump heights were a strain on him. Because of this, we stopped competing in USDAA (United States Dog Agility Association) events, where, at that time, 12 inches was the lowest height allowed.

After that, we competed solely in AKC and NADAC (North American Dog Agility Council) events at the eight-inch (20-cm) jump height level. More recently, we compete in the veteran level in NADAC competition, with a reduced height of just four inches (10 cms).

"When competing in outdoor trials where the grass is not cut short, a small dog's performance can be severely affected. It would be the same as a larger breed running through grass that reached

Barney was the first Dachshund to win the UKC Agility Championship.

his chest! The weather can pose similar problems. Rain and muddy conditions are harder to negotiate for a small dog, and the canvas collapsible tunnel can get quite heavy for the Dachshund to push through.

"Your relationship with the dog is slightly different, too, when training a Dachshund for Agility. Your body language has to be much more animated. Just turning your shoulders to the obstacle you next want the dog to tackle doesn't help a Dachshund that can't see above your shin! Because of this, it takes a longer time to bond as a team. It is very important to work within the dog's sight limitations, and to make the signalling as clear as possible.

SUCCESS AFTER SUCCESS

"Barney has had many highlights in his Agility career. He was the first Dachshund to earn the U-ACH (UKC Agility Championship), and also the first to earn the following AKC Agility titles: NA (Novice Agility), OA (Open Agility), AX

(Excellent Agility), and MX (Master's Agility).

"Barney was the first dog competing in the AKC eight-inch (20-cm) level to earn a MX title, and was just the second dog from the AKC hound group to earn an MX.

"Barney competes in lots of different sports, and has earned titles in Obedience, Field Trials and Earth Dog. At the age of 13, he has also started Tracking!"

KNOW YOUR LIMITS

"Our advice to anyone who might be thinking of taking up Agility is to make sure the Dachshund is in the best shape possible – that means a lean weight, well-trimmed toenails, and a slowly-built-up muscle mass.

"Also remember that, no matter how good your Dachshund is, he will not be able to beat some of the top Agility breeds (Border Collies, Jack Russells, and others). You have to recognise your limitations up front, and enjoy your dog and the time you spend with him."

TRACKING

Tracking is a popular non-competitive outdoor sport where the dog and handler team follow the scent trail made by someone walking earlier in the day. The dog detects a unique combination of smells – the person's body scent, any traces of soap or other toiletries, the scent of their clothes, and the smell of the vegetation crushed underfoot when the scent trail was made.

Tracking could have been invented for the Dachshund. As a scenthound, the Dachshund invariably has his nose to the ground when out on a walk (with his low legs, his nose is nearer to the ground than most breeds), and has a natural ability to follow scent trails. Refining this instinct for Tracking takes time, training and patience, but is a very rewarding experience, where dog and handler work as a close team in the great outdoors.

TRACKING TESTS

In the United States, Tracking is an AKC-recognised sport, with three suffix tracking titles of increasing difficulty – Tracking Dog (TD), Tracking Dog Excellent (TDX), and Variable Surface Tracker (VST) – and one prefix title, Champion Tracker (CT). In the UK, Tracking is one of the components of Working Trials (which also include Obedience and Agility).

SHOWING

The exhibition show world can appear to be a daunting place for someone who doesn't know very much about it. Don't let all the paperwork, rules and regulations put you off, however. Once you have attended a few shows, and spoken with experienced exhibitors, everything will fall into place, and it won't be long before novices are coming to you for advice.

Of course, before you even contemplate showing, you must have a dog that is worthy of being exhibited. An experienced breeder and show person will be able to give you an honest opinion of your dog, so you will know whether it is worthwhile pursuing this hobby. If your dog is not a suitable show specimen, don't despair – you can still enter local fun shows together, which are equally enjoyable and quite inexpensive (showing becomes more costly as you move into Championship shows).

If you are interested in showing your Dachshund, join a local ring-training class (your breed club will have details). There, you will learn how to show your dog to his best advantage, how to move him around the ring and stand him properly. You will also be taught ring procedure, and will be given the opportunity to practise competing. Matches for class members are held on a regular basis.

Show-training classes are of great value to the canine competitors too, socialising them with other dogs and strangers.

Your Dachshund will become relaxed about being handled by lots of different people, and will get used to performing around a variety of dogs. This will prepare him for the noises and distractions that are typical of the show ring.

Lois Ballard from Stratford, Wisconsin, has achieved great success in all areas of training, having titled Dachshunds in all six AKC events open to the breed. Here, she tells how she first got involved in Tracking.

"I have had Dachshunds for 13 years. My parents raised and showed dogs as I was growing up, and I have been going to shows since I was a teenager. I've had several different breeds until I finally discovered the Dachshund. I was considering a smaller breed, something that could sit on your lap to be held, and not make a mess of the house and yard. Dachshunds have the perfect balance of just enough independence while still wanting to please their owner, most of the time.

"I currently have four Miniature Wire-haired Dachshunds. First,

Lois Ballard with Toad.

there's DC Pocketpack Voice Mail MW CD TDX ME OA OAJ VC (also known as Owen), who is my super dog. He is four years old and is one of very few Dachshunds that have earned titles in all six AKC events available for Dachshunds (Showing, Tracking, Agility, Obedience, Field Trials, and Earth Dog).

"Owen loves everyone he meets and does anything I ask of him with all his heart. I have started training him for Variable Surface Tracking (see above). To date, no Dachshund has earned this title, but Owen is doing quite well in his training.

"Owen's mother, DC Sadsack The Cupid Clone MW TD ME VC ROMX, known as Toad, is nine years old. She is more of a specialist than an all-around dog. Her specialty is Field Trialing. She was the Dachshund Club of America's number one Field

ON THE RIGHT TRACK

Trial Merit Dog in 1996 and 1998, and she has passed her ability on to most of her puppies. Toad is a one-person dog, and tracks very well for me, when she wants to. But when there are animal scents around, she would rather hunt than track. Hopefully, she will pass the TDX test before she is too old to try anymore.

"My youngest dog is Toad's daughter, FC Pocketpack Flutter By MW, or Hazel. Hazel is 18 months old and enjoys Agility more than anything else. She is always happy and is Tracking very well. I plan to enter her in a TD test this summer.

"My old dog is Ch. Shoreview Oprah Win For Me MW, known as Oprah, and she is 13.

"Oprah is a shy dog and doesn't like to do anything with strangers watching, so she hasn't competed in any performance events.

"She is devoted to our family and will be with us for the rest of her life.

"I no longer have the Dachshund that I first earned a TDX with, FC Pocketpack Redhead MW TDX, whose pet name was Kitty.

BORN TO TRACK
"Toad passed her TD test and Kitty passed her TDX test on the same day. I was nine months pregnant at the time, and my daughter was born the following weekend. I was at a Field Trial on the Saturday, and came home very early Sunday morning to give birth.

"Some people might think that shows real devotion to my dog activities; others might think I'm just crazy!

GETTING STARTED
"As you can see, I am very involved in Field Trials, where the dog follows the scent of a rabbit. Tracking was suggested to me by a good friend who competes in both activities.

"Since my dogs did well in Field Trials, I

thought they might enjoy Tracking too, so agreed to give it a try.

"My friend laid a very short track for one of my dogs, and, after trying it once, I decided I would like to learn more.

"My interest, in the beginning, was for my dogs to learn to follow a scent trail the best they could and for me to learn to read dog body language better for Field Trial judging. It all developed from there.

MAKING BONDS
"Tracking is a very enjoyable activity, and a close bond develops between dog and handler. Dogs naturally want to be with their people and to please them.

"There's great camaraderie between competitors, too. Being a non-competitive sport, when a dog passes a Tracking test, everyone there congratulates the team, and everyone feels bad when the team fails a test.

"It's not unusual to fail a test, and for the dog to find something that is not meant to be there. I have had encounters with all sorts of creatures, including stray dogs, cats, turtles, fawns, and snakes!"

HOBBY FOR LIFE
"It's important for a breed such as the Dachshund to have a hobby. He is very much a pack dog and sees you as his pack leader – pleasing you pleases the dog.

"I participate in many activities with my dogs, and I think they enjoy them all. It certainly keeps them happy. Every morning, they seem to ask me 'What are we going to do today?'

"Tracking is also great exercise for both the dog and the handler. If you are someone who enjoys spending time outdoors with your Dachshund, Tracking is an ideal activity for you."

Showing is a fascinating hobby, but you need determination to reach the top.

STAND AND DELIVER

Because the Dachshund is a low breed, it is shown on a table (to save everyone's backs when examining and judging the dog!). If you intend to show your puppy, train him to stand on a table from a young age. Never leave a puppy or dog unsupervised on a table, though, as he could seriously injure himself if he were to fall or jump off.

- Stand your Dachshund on a table, and show him a tasty treat in your hand.
- Allow him to gnaw a little of the treat (still holding it in front of him – so that his head is held quite high).
- While the puppy is preoccupied with the treat, with your other hand place the puppy in the show stance. His legs should be straight, with the forelegs parallel to each other, and the hindlegs also parallel to each other.
- When the puppy is in the correct position, say "Stand", give lots of praise, and give him the rest of the treat.
- Practise little and often, but never for prolonged periods or the puppy will grow up to resent being shown. Short sessions will soon teach him the meaning of the word "Stand", and that a treat is in store!

GAIT

For the judge to assess your Dachshund's movement and overall conformation, you will be asked to move your dog around the ring. The judge could ask you to gait your dog up and down the ring in a straight line, or in a triangle shape. When at a trot, the Dachshund should move in a free (not stilted) way. His tail should be carried low, and his head high. Practise a little every day at home or in your garden, so it becomes second nature for you and your Dachshund to find the right pace and move well together.

A SPECIAL BOND

The Dachshund is a very loving breed that thrives on human company. They develop close bonds with their owners, but are also capable of providing friendship and companionship to others.

There are a number of Dachshunds that work as therapy dogs, visiting the elderly, the young, or the sick, in residential homes or hospitals. Many establishments do not allow their patients or residents to have pets, so therapy-dog schemes provide a much-needed service where people can enjoy all the benefits of having a pet without actually owning one.

The therapy dog schemes rely on dedicated dog owners who volunteer their time to share their pets. The dogs are all impeccably behaved and absolutely trustworthy around people, in all situations.

To find out more about such schemes, contact your national kennel club for details of therapy dog organisations, or browse the internet for more information.

A ROSIE FUTURE

Carol Orton has always owned dogs. When her English Setter died in 1995, she fancied a change of breed. Searching for a small, easy-maintenance dog, she decided on the Miniature Smooth Dachshund. Within a few months, she had been bitten by the show bug, and her maintenance-free Dachshund turned into a demanding and time-consuming hobby!

"When I decided on the Dachshund as my new breed, I viewed a recommended litter, and actually came home with two puppies," says Carol, from Staffordshire, England. "I couldn't decide between Heidi and Rosie, so had them both – plus, they were great company for each other.

Rosie, otherwise known as Springborne Rosa-Belle Of Scalamor.

"I first started to think about showing after one or two people said how nice Rosie was. I worked with someone who showed dogs, and she suggested I join a ringcraft (ring-training) club, which I did.

"I also started to visit a few shows, where I got chatting to some of the exhibitors. The Dachshund is a very friendly breed to be involved in. Everyone was really helpful.

"I started show-training Rosie, where I learnt how Rosie should stand and walk around the ring, and how to best show her off to the judge.

"Our first show with Rosie (Springborne Rosa-Belle of Scalamor) was very nerve-wracking, but enjoyable. Although Rosie looked very nice, she was bigger than all the other entrants (Mini Smooths have to be 11lbs/5kgs

and under in the UK). A few exhibitors spoke to me afterwards and gave me some good advice, but I knew it was hopeless pursuing a show career for Rosie because of her size.

"I had bred and shown cats before, and had lots of other dog experience, and decided I would breed from Rosie. I researched her pedigree and the prefixes on it, and took Rosie to an experienced breeder whose line was included on Rosie's pedigree (see Line-breeding, Chapter Eight).

"Rosie had a very good litter, and I kept the smallest female, Lily (Scalamor Lily the Pink). It was then that I became more seriously involved in the show world. Lily was a very pretty dog and did well, first at Open shows, and then Championship shows, and she soon qualified for the world-famous Crufts show.

"Lily has since had a litter, and I have kept one of her sons, Dudley (Scalamor Dudley Nightshade), who qualified for Crufts. I had big hopes early on for Dudley, as he's always been placed high in classes. My instincts were proved right: he won a second at Crufts! As you can imagine, I was absolutely thrilled.

"Showing has gradually become more and more important to me. It takes up a lot of my free time, but I get such a buzz when I go into the ring. I like meeting people who have the same interests, and I love the dogs. My Dachshunds enjoy it, too, especially spending one-to-one time with me, and they genuinely seem to like showing off in the ring!"

HEALING THERAPY

Kitty Johnson has been taking Anna, her Standard Smooth, on therapy dog visits for nearly two years – an arrangement that suits all involved, especially food-obsessed Anna!

"I have been owned by Dachshunds since I was six years old, but when I got Anna (Anna Fantasia) four years ago, it had been a long time since I had a puppy," explains Kitty, from Richmond, Virginia. "Because I wanted a well-behaved dog that I could take travelling to hotels with me, and because Dachshunds are renowned for their stubbornness, we enrolled Anna at a nearby Obedience club, where she trained for the AKC's Canine Good Citizenship test.

"When she passed that course, she was eligible to take the Therapy Dog International test, which is a temperament test for therapy work.

"Anna passed that test, at the age of 18 months, and I then decided it would be nice to visit people in hospitals and other establishments, who miss their dogs and might like a visit to cheer them up.

"I have a rehabilitation hospital two blocks from me and decided that it would be a convenient place to visit. Because it was close, I knew it would be easy to keep visiting once I got started. We have been visiting twice a week for nearly two years now, but Anna has been on maternity leave recently, with a litter of puppies.

Anna: She makes life a little more fun.

"Anna is ideal for therapy dog work. She is small (18 lbs/8kgs), so fits easily on people's laps or on their beds. Since she has a smooth coat, she is easy to keep clean and doesn't affect people who have allergies. Her temperament is very outgoing, so she makes friends with ease.

"Visitors are often surprised to see a dog in a hospital setting. I always ask if they like dogs before approaching a person. But since Anna is small and so cute, people rarely refuse to see her and most patients are delighted to meet her. Dog owners get particularly excited when they see Anna and will talk about dogs they have owned.

"Most patients are in the rehabilitation hospital because of an accident or long-term illness that affects their mobility. They spend six hours a day doing therapy so they can go home. If they can't complete the course, most of them will end up in long-term care, so they try very hard and can become depressed if they do not make progress. Anna cheers them up and makes life a little more fun.

"Many times, I come in during the afternoon therapy sessions when the therapists use Anna to encourage a patient to complete a series of exercises. The pay-off is time with Anna!

"Anna enjoys her visits enormously – all Dachshunds love food and the patients give Anna treats that I take with me. But she also likes the excitement of all the different sights, sounds, smells, and new people."

CHAPTER SEVEN

THE WORKING TECKEL

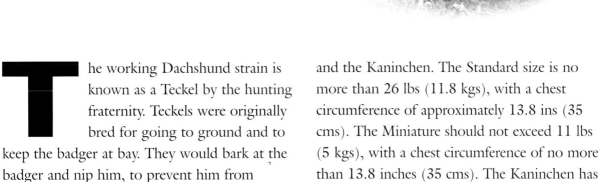

The working Dachshund strain is known as a Teckel by the hunting fraternity. Teckels were originally bred for going to ground and to keep the badger at bay. They would bark at the badger and nip him, to prevent him from digging further down. In the meantime, the handler would dig out the badger.

Today, this sport is illegal in many countries. Some allow hunting of fox and rabbit, and blood-trailing for dead or wounded deer and wild boar. Research the laws that apply to your country (your national Teckel club, or Dachshund club that specialises in hunting will be able to advise you). If you don't wish to hunt live animals, you could get involved in Tracking scents instead – training your Dachshund to track a family member can be great fun, and useful too, if you lose one of them on a walk!

SIZE
Teckels come in three sizes: Standard, Miniature, and the Kaninchen. The Standard size is no more than 26 lbs (11.8 kgs), with a chest circumference of approximately 13.8 ins (35 cms). The Miniature should not exceed 11 lbs (5 kgs), with a chest circumference of no more than 13.8 inches (35 cms). The Kaninchen has no weight category, but has a chest circumference of 11.8 ins (30 cms) maximum.

Standard
The Standard is worked on all legal game, and is able to hunt a wide variety of animals, ranging in size from a field mouse to tracking down wild boar and deer by blood-trailing. They dig and go to ground on fox and rabbit quite readily, and will flush out pheasant and reluctant-to-move grouse from dense thickets.

Miniature
Miniatures dig and go to ground on rabbits and small vermin, and will flush out game birds from dense cover.

Kaninchen

The Kaninchen is worked on rabbits and small vermin.

COATS

There are three recognised coats in Teckels: Wire-haired, Smooth-haired and Long-haired.

Smooth-haired

Smooth-haired Teckels are easy to clean and dry down after a day's work. It is easy to assess their skeletal conformation as it is not masked by the coat.

Long-haired

The Long-hair should have a thick, soft coat covering the body, running into silky feathering on the ears, legs and tail. Long-haired Teckels often have longer legs than their show counterparts, and are particularly successful in water, retrieving duck.

The true Wire-haired coat (left), and the smoother Pinwire coat (right).

Wire-haired

Unfortunately, the Wire coat is not a stable characteristic, and four variations occur, sometimes all in one litter.

Wire-hair

The true Wire-hair has a stiff, harsh coat, wiry to the touch, lying close to the body, but noticeably more profuse on the muzzle and legs. This type of coat does not need stripping to achieve correctness.

Pinwire

The Pinwire is genetically the same as a true Wire, but, in the Pinwire, the recessive Smooth has a greater effect on the Wire genes. These dogs can look virtually Smooth, but the giveaway is whiskery hairs on the jaw and legs, and sometimes along the centre of the back.

Woolly

When the Wire coat is inherited in a double dose, the resulting offspring will appear with a soft fluffy coat, which needs to be stripped out to achieve correctness.

Recessive Smooth

Smooth-haired puppies appear in litters even when both parents are Wire-haired. They are valuable to breeding programmes (when bred to the woolly coat) to keep Wire coats harsh and bristly. They are not permitted by national kennel clubs, but are useful for working litters.

TRAINING

Teckels can be very stubborn and wilful, so training your puppy for obedience is essential before starting more formal earth dog training. Training should always be fun: if you treat a Teckel too harshly, he will never work for you. The dog's field name should be short and sharp.

GENERAL OBEDIENCE

The dog is walked to heel on the left side if you are a right-handed shooter, or on the right-hand side if you are left-handed. Once lead-walking is achieved, the dog should walk to heel off-lead too (see page 74).

Deer dogs should be taught to walk three-quarters of their length in front of you. This is so that you can look at your dog closely for any signs that he has picked up a scent – he will become very alert, sniff the air, and adopt a pointing position. He may also stand still and shiver from head to foot. Make sure the dog walks at your pace. If he pulls, tug the lead and say "Heel" to bring him back. Never walk a dog off the lead in traffic, no matter how well he is trained.

SOCIALISATION

Working dogs must be socialised to all livestock: ferrets, sheep, poultry, cattle and horses, all animals they would encounter in the countryside. Introduce your Teckel puppy to these animals as soon as he has completed his vaccinations.

Walk your puppy through a farmyard (first

seeking permission) and, if the puppy shows any hint of excessive excitement, tell him "No" firmly, and bring him in to heel. Repeated exposure to animals will soon remove the novelty, and your Teckel should grow up without giving livestock a second glance.

GUNFIRE

A dog should be brought up to loud noises before his ears are opened. Teckel breeders will clap their hands near the puppies and bang food dishes. At about 12 to 14 weeks old, the pup should be subjected to the use of a starter pistol being fired at a distance of about 30 metres (98.5 feet). Distance is an important factor, as it is easy to ruin a dog by frightening him.

As the pup gets older, reduce the distance until you are firing over the dog by the time he is six months old. Introduction to live gunfire should not be taught until the Teckel is around nine months old. Remember: never fire when the dog is standing in front of you, as you could damage his ears.

DEER TRAILING

Many Teckels are used by deerstalkers for finding wounded or dead deer. Although shot through the heart and clinically dead, a deer can frequently run 140 metres (460 feet) before going down. The body is found by means of blood-trailing. It is illegal in most countries to stalk deer without a trained dog, where the practice is permitted at all.

Going to ground to hunt rabbits and other small animals is second nature to Teckels, so, if

Going to ground is second nature to a Teckel.

you are planning to work your Teckel on deer, it is advisable for the dog to be used for that type of hunting alone. He can be put to other game after one or two seasons, depending on the amount of deer experience he has gained. Once his deer training is consolidated, he can be introduced to fox and rabbit (according to each country's laws).

Blood-trailing training can begin when your Teckel is as young as four months old. It should not be practised any more than twice a week or the pup will become bored with it.

LAYING TRACKS

You must always use cold blood for training (your hunting club will advise of a local supplier). If you start your Teckel on warm blood or live animals, the dog will be following the scent of the adrenaline, as well as the blood. Then, if you require the dog to track cold blood or a dead animal, he may not be able to, as the adrenaline scent will not be present.

Always lay the blood trail downwind so that the scent is going away from you. Keep your foot scent and the blood scent separate, as you want the dog to follow the blood scent – not you. If possible, leave your dog at home when laying the trail.

A continuous trail of blood is laid on short grass to about 20 metres (66 feet). At the end of the trail, put a small piece of liver on to a deerskin that is kept in the freezer for this purpose.

GETTING STARTED

A dog harness with a pair of hawking bells attached should always be used for blood-trailing. The bells (available from suppliers of falconry equipment) can be heard up to half a mile (0.8 kms) away, and ensure you cannot lose your dog. In time, your dog will associate the sound of the bells with 'work', thus helping him to focus.

When first training, attach a lead to the harness and show your Teckel the blood trail. If he strays off the trail, pull him back, telling him, in an excited tone, to "Find the deer". Once the dog has successfully completed the trail, he is

The dog must get used to a range of terrain.

rewarded with a piece of liver. You can then start increasing the difficulty of the trail – by making the distance longer, changing direction, and, eventually, moving on to woodland trails, which are harder to track.

GROUND COVER

It is helpful for the trainer to accustom the dog to a range of different terrain. Walk the puppy in long grass, bracken, or any other soft cover, then bramble and dense thickets will come more easily to the dog later on.

LIVE TRAINING

At about eight to nine months of age, your Teckel should be ready for his first hunting season, depending on how much training he has achieved. Do not start hunting until your dog is absolutely ready. If in doubt, continue training.

CLUBS

For details of your nearest Teckel Club, contact your national breed organisation or club.

FIELD TRIALS

In the United States, the Dachshund's working ability is tested in a Field Trial, where each Dachshund is judged on his accuracy in following the trail, his co-operation with his brace mate, his responsiveness to the handler, and his willingness to enter brush (heavy ground cover) to follow the trail.

Handlers with dogs competing in the first matches (braces) wait in the field, while the other participants form a brush-beating line and move across the field in search of rabbits, calling "Tally-ho" when one is spotted. Competing dogs are then placed on the rabbit's trail once it is out of sight. The intention of the trial is that the dogs follow the scent trail – they are not meant to kill or injure the rabbit.

Once all the competitors have run, the highest-scoring dogs run again in the second series, where dogs compete directly against their brace mate for a win or lose position. Subsequent series are called until each Dachshund has been defeated by the Dachshund placed immediately above him.

MAKING OF A CHAMPION

There are three 'stakes' or classes:
• Open all-age dogs
• Open all-age bitches
• Field Champions.
Points are earned towards a Field Championship title, with placements in the Open Stakes. The number of points earned is based on the number of entries in the class, and the

FIELD OF DREAMS

David and Cheri Faust purchased their first Dachshund, Abby (Little Abigail Ginger Snap CG CGC ME) in 1989, and have contributed to their Dachsie numbers considerably since then. They currently have 30 Mini Smooths, all house dogs and members of the Faust family. Such a large number of dogs certainly doesn't mean any individuals are neglected – David and Cheri have trained all the dogs to a high standard in a number of different disciplines, including Field Trials.

"We love the Dachshund's big-dog attitude in a small-dog package," say David and Cheri, from Madison, Wisconsin, USA. "They have a total devotion and loyalty to their family and very amusing personalities – Dachshunds are the only dogs in the world for us!

"We learned about Field Trials through the Badger Dachshund Club, of which we were members. Many of the friends we had made

Butch (Field Champion Longtime's Woodland Marauder).

through the club were involved in Field Trials, so we attended a trial to see what it was all about. We really wanted to be involved in doing something with our dogs. We were beginning to participate in conformation shows, but had not yet had much success.

FIRST TIME LUCKY

"Sarah (FC Longtime's Sable Serenade MS) was the first dog we entered in a Field Trial in May, 1993. We were very nervous, and it was a good thing Sarah was a natural at the sport. She was Next Best Qualified after the four dogs that received placements, in a stake of 30 entries. There's nothing that will get you hooked on something like a little success – we became avid field trialers then and there! We entered 8 Trials that year, and now attend about 20 annually.

SPECIAL MOMENTS

"We feel successful every time one of the dogs has a 'good run'; and there are plenty of days where that sense of pride is all we take home – judging is subjective and is also based on how well the other dogs run on that day.

"We have had some very special moments over the years: earning our first Field Championship (Butch – FC Longtime's Woodland Marauder Butch); earning our first Dual Championship (Claire – Dual Ch. Longtime's Tender is the Night); and earning our first placement in the Field Champion stake (Butch). We were very proud of Butch being Number Five Field Champion in 1998 under the Dachshund Club of America Merit Point System.

"We earned our first Absolute in 1998. One of the Trials we were competing in was unable to finish with the Absolute run at the end of the day (in the Absolute run, the Dog Stake winner, the Bitch Stake winner, and the Field Champion Stake winner compete against each other). The decision was made to run Absolute the following weekend at another trial. Butch had won his first Field Champion Stake and therefore was eligible to run for Absolute.

"The following weekend, our Field Champion Jack (FC Longtime's Jack of Diamonds) won the Field Champion Stake, and then won Absolute at the end of the Trial. The following morning, the Absolute run from the Trial that hadn't been completed was held, and Butch won Absolute for that Trial. Since it was Cheri's birthday, we told everyone that our boys gave her those Absolutes as a birthday present!

"One of our greatest successes came at the Dachshund Club of America National Field Trial in 2000. Butch had been placed 2nd in the Field Champion Stake at the Field Trial hosted by the Dachshund Club of Santa Ana Valley. The next day, at the National Field Trial, Butch was placed 1st in the Field Champion Stake, and went on to win Absolute.

ENJOYMENT

"The dogs love using their noses and chasing game. I also think they enjoy doing something that pleases us so much. For a Dachshund, being able to do both of these things at the same time – hunting and pleasing us – is heaven itself.

"The whole atmosphere at a Field Trial is ideal for people who enjoy spending time with their dogs and other people. There is lots of time to spend outdoors, walking with people, and talking about upcoming events, pedigrees, puppies, training, and general 'dog talk', which we enjoy.

"We really like seeing the dogs use their natural ability to trail game and never cease to wonder at their scenting abilities. There's a great sense of satisfaction from spending time with the dogs and learning to work in co-operation with them. The social aspect is something we both enjoy, too, but most of all, we love how much the dogs love it!"

placement in the class. Currently, 35 points, one first-place, and placements at a minimum of three trials is the requirement for the Field Champion title.

TRAINING

Initial training can begin with puppies by socialising them around people and other dogs, encouraging them to be independent when walking loose in a fenced-in area, and to come when called (see Chapter Three).

- Use a canvas dummy that has had bottled rabbit scent liberally applied to it. (Training scent is available at many sporting-goods stores or by mail-order from hunting-supplies catalogues.)
- Drag it in a line, for the puppy to follow the track.
- When the dog finds the dummy at the end of the line, make a game out of it. Give lots of praise and play a game. This gets the dog excited about finding his 'quarry'.
- The line is made progressively more difficult by putting turns in the trail (see Tracking, page 82), and by dragging the line over different types of cover, such as dead leaves, green grass, and marsh grass.
- Some trainers use a dead rabbit (kept in the freezer for such purposes), which prepares the Dachshund for moving on to working in a field with live rabbits to hunt. If a dead rabbit is used, do not use a constant line when trailing it on the ground – lift it up for the odd step (to simulate the track of a hopping rabbit).

The Earth Dog must enter a tunnel and seek out the quarry.

EARTH DOG

The Dachshund's original function, in the early days of his history, was to go to ground and alert his handler to the presence of quarry. While waiting for the owner to arrive at the scene, the Dachshund was expected to bark and nip at the quarry. This would keep the quarry focused on the dog, rather than attempting to escape.

Earth Dog is a sport that tests these same skills in the breed. It is particularly popular in the United States, where it is an AKC-recognised sport, with titles available. There is some interest in the activity in the UK, but it is very much in its early stages.

The dog is tested in underground tunnels to go to caged rats at the end and show aggression for the hunt. The rats are never released from the cage, and so are not killed or injured by the dogs. The aim of Earth Dog competition is to show how bold the dog is in spirit, not to test his rat-killing skills.

Each dog is scored and timed, and works

toward different titles: Junior Earth Dog (JE), Senior Earth Dog (SE), and Master Earth Dog (ME). The complexity of the dens increases as the dog progresses in his Earth Dog career.

For example, introductory tests contain one 90-degree turn in the underground tunnel, whereas a Master Earth Dog test will be more demanding, with an entrance that is not readily visible (blocked with a removable obstruction), a false den entrance to confuse the dog, an obstruction within one of the tunnels, and three 90-degree turns.

In each instance, the dog is expected to enter a tunnel, seek out the quarry, and bark, growl and dig at the cage to show he is interested in the prey. The dog must begin to work quarry within two minutes from the time he enters the earth, and must work for 30 seconds to qualify. A dog must qualify under two different judges to earn his Junior Earth Dog title, and then he works his way up from there.

To find out more, contact your national kennel club or breed club for information on any Earth Dog clubs in your area.

TUNNEL VISION

Jean Jasinsky from Britt, Minnesota, has been involved in Dachshunds since 1956. She has Miniature Smooth- and Long-haired Dachsies, and loves nothing more than training them for Earth Dog events to give them an opportunity to indulge in their natural instincts.

"I first became involved while at a show where the Minnesota Dachshund Club put on a demonstration. I was hooked.

"The club held a workshop for interested owners, and I took along Pi (Am/Can Ch. Duchwood's Cedarhurst Pi), who was seven months old at the time. He loved it.

"So I made artificial tunnels and a rat cage, got old dirty rat bedding and made scent for the den. We use rat urine and faeces, which is watered down a little and set in the sun to get it really foul-smelling. I dug up one of my pastures and put tunnels in according to the American Kennel Club rules, and several interested owners and dogs joined in.

"Sometimes the dogs follow the scent and go to ground, but come out too soon – unsure of how long the tunnel is.

"They have only 30 seconds to get to the quarry, so might not always qualify. But do they care? No. They have a brilliant time whether they win, lose, or draw!

"The dogs really enjoy the work. They love to use their noses to dig and to hunt, and let you know they are enjoying themselves by barking with joy.

"For me, it offers a good day out, meeting up with like-minded people, where we just talk about dogs all day long!"

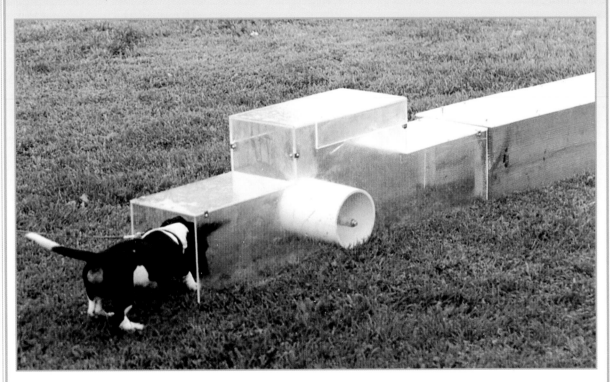

Pi: A complete natural when it comes to Earth Dog work.

CHAPTER EIGHT

SEEKING PERFECTION

Each breed of dog, recognised by a national kennel club, has a Breed Standard. This is best described as a written blueprint, detailing in words what the ideal specimen for each breed should look like.

Coat, size, skeletal structure, colour, and temperament are all described, giving breeders an ideal to work towards, and judges a model of perfection so they can evaluate the dogs that are being exhibited.

The Standard means that changing fashions should not permanently alter a breed (at least, that's the theory), and ensures that each breed remains distinct and true.

Full copies of the Dachshund's Breed Standard are available from your national kennel club, but here is a brief summary of the most pertinent points of the English and American Breed Standards.

BREED STANDARD

General appearance

The Dachshund is best described as long and low – a long body that is close to the ground. He has a muscular body, and appears bold and intelligent.

Characteristics

A working dog, suited to going to ground, the Dachshund has well-developed senses, and a particularly good nose. This is a determined worker, renowned for his perseverance. Lively and spirited, this intelligent dog is brave to the point of rashness, despite his diminutive size.

Temperament

A loyal dog, the Dachshund is adaptable and good-tempered. It is rare ever to encounter a shy Dachshund; most are bold and outgoing.

The Dachshund has a long muscular body that is close to the ground.

Head and Skull

The head, like the body, is long, and gradually narrows to the tip of the nose. The skull is slightly arched, and slopes gently into the muzzle, which is also arched slightly. The stop (the indentation between the eyes) is barely noticeable, and not at all prominent. The jaw bones are strong, and the mouth is able to open wide – again useful. This would have been developed for the breed's Earth Dog work when the Dachshund would have been expected to nip his quarry (see Chapters One and Six). The lips are well stretched, and cover the lower jaw.

Eyes

A Dachshund's almond-shaped, medium-sized eyes are entrancing. They should be as dark as possible, though chocolate Dachshunds can have lighter-coloured eyes. 'Wall' (blue) eyes are acceptable only in dapples.

Ears

The broad, pendulous ears are placed quite high on the head, allowing sounds to be heard easily. They are rounded, and the tips touch the edge of the dog's cheeks (apart from when alerted to sounds, when the mobile ears may move around, radar-like).

Mouth

A working Earth Dog requires a powerful mouth, and the Dachshund is no exception. The teeth and jaws should be strong, set in a scissor bite. This is where the top teeth closely overlap the bottom ones, ensuring that the teeth can grip strongly when needed.

The dark eyes, pendulous ears and powerful mouth are typical of the breed.

Neck

The perfect Dachshund neck is long (isn't everything on a Dachshund?) and muscular. The skin should fit well – there should be no evidence of loose skin hanging around the neck or throat.

Slightly arched, the neckline flows effortlessly down to the dog's shoulders.

Forequarters

The forequarters are strong and muscular, so vital in a successful Earth Dog that needs to dig earth and pull himself forward through narrow tunnels, using his forequarters.

To achieve this strength, the shoulder blades are long and wide, and set at a 45-degree angle on the rib cage, thus providing excellent leverage.

Body

The Dachshund body is long and well muscled. The shoulders slope down to the dog's back, which should be straight. A dog whose back sags in the middle, with his stomach nearly touching the floor, is not acceptable! The body should be sufficiently clear of the ground to allow free movement. The chest should be very prominent, providing plenty of lung room for energetic work.

Hindquarters

Like the forequarters, the hindquarters are strong and well muscled. When viewed from behind, the straight hindlegs are parallel – but not too close – to each other.

Feet

The front feet are particularly important for digging and clawing through tunnels. They are broad (providing a 'shovel' effect), and compact. The hind feet are smaller. The toes on all four feet are arched, and have strong nails. The pads are thick, so providing the dog with tough 'work boots'.

Tail

The tail follows on directly from the spine. It is carried fairly level – never too high or too low.

Gait/Movement

The Dachshund should move in a fluid, effortless – but powerful – way, thanks to his well-muscled limbs and bone construction. When seen from the front or the rear, the Kennel Club requires the limbs to be parallel with each other; the American Kennel Club states that a slight incline is permissible, and that a parallel position is difficult to achieve given the shortness of leg, and the width of chest.

Coat

- Smooth-haired: a short, shining, dense, smooth coat. The underside of the tail has thicker 'bristle-type' hairs. The ears should be well covered, not leathery.
- Long-haired: the coat is long and straight (or slightly wavy). The hair is longer on the chest, on the underside of the body, and on the back of the legs. Although profuse, the coat should not hide the dog's structure. The

Miniatures are weighed at the ringside to ensure they conform to the Breed Standard's stipulations.

greatest length of hair is on the tail, where it is carried gracefully like a flag. The ears should be well feathered.

- Wire-haired: a short, rough outercoat, with a soft, dense undercoat. The ears have smoother, less coarse hair. Longer hair forms on the chin (producing a 'beard'), and bushy eyebrows.

Colour

All colours are allowed – red, black, chocolate, grey (blue), fawn (Isabella), and wild boar (brown or grey with a black stripe down the back, and brindled sides). As well as whole colours (where the dog is one colour), there are also two-coloured Dachshunds, which have tan markings, such as black and tan, and chocolate and tan. A dappled (mottled) coat and a brindle (striped) coat also exist. In the United States, white patches are permissible.

Size

In the UK Standard, the size is stated as 9-12 kgs (20-26 lbs). In the United States, the weight range is larger, at around 16-32 lbs (7.26-14.5 kgs).

Miniatures

In the UK, Standard and Miniature Dachshunds have separate classes, but, in the United States, they are judged together. In the UK, the ideal weight is 4.5 kgs (10 lbs). Prizes in the show ring should not be given to dogs weighing more than 5 kgs (11 lbs). In the US, Miniatures compete in a class for dogs "11 lbs and under at 12 months of age and older".

UNDERSTANDING PEDIGREES

A pedigree is a dog's family tree, detailing his ancestors. It is an important document, that experienced breeders can use to their advantage.

Combining a detailed knowledge of the breeding stock available, and of the principles involved in genetics, a breeder can use pedigrees to pinpoint breeding patterns. They can discover which males or females consistently produce winners, for example, or which dogs may be responsible for health problems.

Once a breeder has assessed his stock, his conclusions will determine his method of breeding.

IN-BREEDING

In-breeding involves breeding close relatives, such as siblings. It is difficult to achieve good results, for not only are qualities increased, the likelihood of doubling up on faults is also increased. However, it can be successfully used by highly experienced breeders.

Breeders Mr and Mrs Earles were long-term admirers of the Swansford dogs. When they decided to breed with their bitch, Sheasdac Starr Shine, they were aware of the Swansford line on her sire's side, and sought the expert advice of the owners of the Swansford dogs (Margaret Swann and Daniel Roberts). As a result, Ch. Dandydayo Trouble Maker of Swansford was mated to Sheasdac Starr Shine, his half-sister (both sharing the same father). As a result, a lovely litter was produced, including Ch. Earlsdac Pollyanna.

Ch. Earlsdac Pollyanna: An example of in-breeding.

Parents	Grandparents	Great-Grandparents	Great-Great-Grandparents
Ch. Dandydayo Trouble Maker of Swansford	Ch. Swansford Kamador	Ch. Swansford Jymador	Ch. Swansford EL. Kommador
			Ch. Frankanwen Gold Charm of Swansford
		Ch. Swansford ZsaZsadora	Ch. Skywalker Self Raising Sid
			Swansford Kistadora
	Swansford Magiadora	Ch. Swansford EL. Kommador	Ch. Swansford Kommador
			Swansford Zeldora
		Sweet Sensation of Swansford	Ch. Frankanwen Mandrille
			Ch. Frankanwen Gold Charm of Swansford
Sheasdac Starr Shine	Ch. Swansford Kamador	Ch. Swansford Jymador	Ch. Swansford EL. Kommador
			Ch. Frankanwen Gold Charm of Swansford
		Ch. Swansford ZsaZsadora	Ch. Skywalker Self Raising Sid
			Swansford Kistadora
	Rubylans Gwendolene Lucy of Sheasdac	Hoyjac Harvester	Ch. Africandawns Yank Go Home
			Frankanwen Abba
		Baladawn Lilac Lady of Rubylans	Katelyn Consolidator of Baladawn
			Spanish Silver of Bonavia

LINE-BREEDING

If a breeder is consistently producing good dogs of sound temperament, with no health problems, he may decide to breed distant relatives with each other in order that the qualities are replicated. This is known as line-breeding.

'Flossie', bred by Ms Thomas, is a good example of a line-bred Champion, with her parents both sharing two common ancestors (Ch. Woodheath Lunar Eclipse and NZ Ch. Burntbarn Crackerjack).

Ch. Shenaligh Candy Floss: An example of line-breeding.

Parents	Grandparents	Great-Grandparents	Great-Great-Grandparents
Woodheath Sausalito	Ch. Southcliff San Fransiscan	Ch. Brigmerston Sir Francis	Brigmerston Ravenhead Eamon
			Ch. Brigmerston Loop De Loop
		Ch. Southcliffe Sweet Music	Ch. Southcliff Salvatore
			Sunara Golden Melody of Southcliffe
	Ch. Woodheath Lunar Eclipse	NZ Ch. Burntbarn Crackerjack	Mertynabbot Bingo
			Burntbarn Adah
		Woodheath Lunar Lady	Minutist Postiche
			Woodheath Lively Lady
Ch. Shenaligh Vanity Fair	Ch. Rhinestar Dedication	Ch. Sunara Sorrento	Sunara Mertynabbot Goblin
			Imber Demi Tasse
		Woodreed Little Blessing	Ch. Woodreed Little Footman
			Rodell Sea Coral
	Woodheath Lady Aureole	Woodheath Wellington	Ch. Woodheath Bismark
			Woodheath Tanya
		Ch. Woodheath Lunar Eclipse	NZ Ch. Burntbarn Crackerjack
			Woodheath Lunar Lady

OUT-CROSSING

This type of breeding includes the mating of entirely unrelated animals. Flo won 16 Kennel Club Challenge Certificates, 9 Reserve CCs, 13 Best of Breeds, and 2 Reserve Best of Hound Groups.

Breeder and owner Jean Forster used out-crossing because she had always admired Smart Alec (the sire), and considered that he had the ideal qualities she was looking for as a stud for Geffle's Minuet (Flo's dam). "You can't keep going to the same line for a prolonged period of time," says Jean. "You have to bring in a new dog occasionally, and Smart Alec was an excellent all-rounder who had produced good dogs in the past."

Ch. Geffle's Floella: An example of out-crossing.

Parents	Grandparents	Great-Grandparents	Great-Great-Grandparents
Ch. Wingcrest Smart Alec	Hobbithill Lorgan of Wingcrest	Ch. Jubilee Gift of Wingcrest	Ch. Hobbithill Fescue of Wingcrest
			Gay Courtisan of Wingcrest
		Ch. Nymphean of Hobbithill	Ch. Braishvale Cracker Jack
			Bluebell of Hobbithill
	Ch. Likely Lass of Wingcrest	Ch. Jubilee Gift of Wingcrest	Ch. Hobbithill Fescue of Wingcrest
			Gay Courtisan of Wingcrest
		Station House Silver Charm	Eastville Silver Sinbad
			Eastville Jewel
Geffles Minuet	Berrycourt Black Reilly	Ch. Berrycourt Blackthorn	Ch. Braishvale Cracker Jack
			Berrycourt Morning Star
		Berrycourt Sweet Charity	Ch. Berrycourt Robin
			Berrycourt True Song
	Geffles Lucretia	Hylows Red Ringleader of Sauminda	Ch. Pipersvale Pina Colada
			Hylowes Martina Miraculous
		Geffles Bonnie Lass	Geffles Vincent
			Geffles Angel Delight

PUPPY TO CHAMPION

'Monty' pictured at six weeks.

Eleven months.

Fully mature: A Champion, and a top sire.

The transformation of an eight-week-old puppy through to a fully-grown adult is nothing short of a miracle. From a waddling little puppy, through the ugly duckling stage between seven and ten months, and finally on to maturity, the Dachshund develops his coat, as well as his skeleton and size.

Often, the seeds of a great Champion can be seen at an early stage, as this series of photos shows. Pictured is British and Irish Champion Ablebody Pizzicato (Monty) from six weeks of age through to adulthood. Monty gained his first Challenge Certificate, and won Best of Breed at Crufts, at the age of three, and hasn't stopped winning since! He has not been shown excessively, but has 11 CCs and 6 Reserve CCs to his credit.

CHAPTER NINE

HEALTH CARE

The Dachshund is a hardy breed, designed to withstand sometimes harsh conditions. However, his working background and conformation (in particular his long back) does predispose him to certain complaints, particularly spinal injuries. This chapter will give you details of the more common breed-associated conditions (see page 120) that you should be aware of. First, however, we will look at the important subject of preventative health care.

PREVENTATIVE CARE

Responsible veterinary care is aimed at disease prevention. This involves:
• An adequate vaccination programme.
• Parasite control programmes.
• Controlled exercise sufficient to satisfy your pet's needs. However, overexercise, in the young animal especially, can result in joint

and bone abnormalities (see Chapters Two and Four).
• Grooming – not only combing and brushing, but also attention to ears, eyes, teeth and so on, during which time problems can be detected, hopefully before they develop into anything too serious (see Chapter Five).
• Training – Dachshunds, no matter whether Standards or Minis, can be very pushy little dogs and training should start as soon as you acquire the puppy, often before vaccinations have commenced (see Chapter Three).

VACCINATION

Vaccination and inoculation are, for our purposes, synonymous terms. Vaccination subjects the body to micro-organisms to stimulate immunity. In order that the micro-organisms do not cause disease, they have to be altered, either killed (inactivated) or weakened (attenuated). As long as the micro-organisms are introduced into the body, any method can be

used – for example, vaccination against kennel cough (infectious tracheitis) is carried out by the administration of nasal drops.

Inoculation involves introduction of the agent into the tissues of the body and is usually by injection. This stimulates the body to produce an active immunity that lasts a variable time according to the vaccine and the disease.

Early Immunity

Puppies are born with an immunity that they acquire initially from the mother while still in the womb. The necessary antibodies cross the placenta from the mother's bloodstream to that of the puppies. They only last about three weeks, but are topped up by further antibodies secreted in the milk and passed to the puppy while nursing. This is called passive immunity and, once weaning begins, the protection wanes in three to four weeks.

Primary vaccination should be carried out as soon as the passive immunity has declined sufficiently to allow the puppy to respond to the vaccine. This is the danger period for the puppy, since he is not only susceptible to the vaccine but is equally susceptible to any natural virus, and can thus develop the disease.

Vaccine manufacturers constantly strive to develop vaccines that will stimulate the puppy to build up a solid, active immunity even in the face of circulating maternal antibodies.

Today, there are licensed vaccines available that can be completed by 10-12 weeks of age, affording the puppy a solid immunity. Socialisation and training can therefore commence that much earlier.

Discuss with your veterinarian the vaccines used, and explain that you would like a solid protection for your puppy as early as possible in order that you can socialise him.

Booster Vaccinations

Vaccination does not give lifelong immunity; reinforcement (boosting) will be required. Recent work indicates that the amount of immunity conferred varies with the disease and whether the vaccine is attenuated or inactivated. Generally, killed vaccines confer a much shorter length of protection.

Most canine vaccines today are multivalent, that is, they cover several diseases. This is for reasons of both cost and convenience. Some components, particularly those giving protection against leptospirosis, are inactivated. With a multivalent vaccine, the efficacy of the product as a whole is considered in relation to the shortest period of effective protection. Thus, although it is likely that protection against diseases such as distemper and hepatitis will last for much longer than a year, because these are combined with Leptospirosis, the manufacturer's recommendations will be that an annual booster of the multivalent vaccine is advised.

There is concern among dog owners today that over-vaccination can result in serious reactions, but, in four decades of busy canine practice, I have never had to treat a dog with a serious vaccine reaction. Therefore, I would err on the side of safety and of over-protection rather than under-protection.

Immunity acquired from the dam wanes as weaning gets underway.

If you have any concerns, queries or questions, discuss these with your vet at the time of the primary vaccination.

Measuring Immunity

Blood tests are available, both for puppies and adult dogs, that will accurately indicate whether an adequate level of protection is present in that animal, thus indicating whether revaccination is necessary. However, the cost of establishing the level of circulating antibodies against one disease is likely to be more than a combined vaccine against all the diseases. Also, your Dachshund, with his independent nature and notoriously difficult-to-find veins, is unlikely to be exactly unfazed by repeated blood tests! Plus, the breed has short legs and a good nose. Because he is low to the ground and forever sniffing, he is

likely to pick up any infection that happens to be around.

Types Of Vaccine

In the United States, vaccines tend to be classified as core vaccines and non-core vaccines. Core vaccines protect against diseases that are serious, fatal, or difficult to treat. In the UK, these include distemper, parvovirus and adenovirus (hepatitis). In the United States, rabies is also included and this well may be so in the UK in the near future as a result of the change in the quarantine laws.

Non-core vaccines include those against bordetellosis, Leptospirosis (kidney disease), coronavirus (which causes diarrhoea, especially in puppies), and borrelia (Lyme disease). Lyme disease is a tick-borne disease that is of considerable importance in North America and does also occur in the UK. A vaccine is available in North America, (currently not licensed in the UK) and it is known to cause reactions in a number of dogs.

Canine Distemper

This once universal canine killer disease is now relatively rare in most developed western countries, mainly due to vaccination. Symptoms include fever, diarrhoea, coughing, and discharges from the nose and eyes. Sometimes the pads harden, a sign of the so-called 'hardpad' variant. Further signs include seizures, muscle-twitching, and paralysis. The virus can also be involved in the kennel cough (infectious tracheitis) syndrome.

Hepatitis

Also known as adenovirus disease, signs range from sudden death with the peracute infection, to mild cases where the dog appears only to be a bit 'off-colour'. Common symptoms include fever, enlargement of all the lymph nodes (glands), and a swollen liver.

During recovery, 'blue eye' can occur. This is due to the swelling of the cornea (the clear part in front of the eye) which makes the dog appear blind. Although initially very worrying, this usually resolves quickly without impairing the sight.

Rabies

This is an extremely serious zoonotic disease (meaning it is communicable to humans). It is present on all continents except Australasia and Antarctica. Some countries, however, including the UK, are free of the disease. This usually is due to geographical barriers; for example, the British Isles are surrounded by water.

The virus is spread through bites from infected animals, particularly foxes in Europe, and stray dogs in other parts of the world.

Vaccination is mandatory in many countries, including the United States. At present in Britain, although rabies vaccines are now freely available, they are only mandatory if you wish to take your dog to certain authorised countries and rabies-free islands and return under the PETS travel scheme.

Parvovirus

The usual signs of parvo infection include:

sudden vomiting and diarrhoea, which is often blood-stained. Treatment, as with all viral diseases, is mainly supportive, and rapid fluid replacement therapy can certainly be life-saving.

The disease first appeared in 1978 and achieved worldwide distribution by the 1980s. As a result of the development of safe, effective vaccines, the disease has been brought under control, although it is still a serious killer disease of dogs, rivalling only that of distemper in many parts of the world.

Vaccination of the young puppy is recommended. Modern vaccines are effective even in the face of circulating maternal antibodies, so puppies can be inoculated as early as six weeks of age.

Leptospirosis

Unlike the other components of multivalent vaccines, Leptospira organisms are bacteria, not viruses. Two forms are important in dogs: Leptospira canicola (mainly transmitted in the urine of infected dogs) and Leptospira icterohaemorrhagae (for which rats are the main vectors).

Leptospirosis, which is communicable to humans, poses a particular problem to Dachshunds, due to their fondness for rat-catching. Country dogs, if in contact with infected waterways, are also at risk.

The type of Leptospirosis spread by rats is by far the most devastating to the dog and usually results in jaundice, then death from liver and/or kidney failure. However, unlike the viral diseases, treatment with the use of antibiotics is

Leptospirosis is spread by rats, so protection for Dachshunds is vital.

effective, provided it is instituted early in the course of the disease. Again, vaccination is by far the wisest course, with regular boosting as recommended.

Parainfluenza

A component against parainfluenza virus has been incorporated in multivalent vaccines for some years. This is due to the fact that this virus is considered to be the primary causal agent in the kennel cough syndrome (infectious tracheitis) in North America. However, in the UK, the bacterium Bordetella bronchiseptica is considered to be the main cause. Yearly revaccination is advised by the manufacturers, with the suggestion that, if your dog is going into a high-risk situation (e.g. going to a boarding kennel, attending shows, or going into any high concentration of dogs), even earlier revaccination should be considered.

Bordetellosis

The kennel cough syndrome, or infectious tracheitis, can spread like wildfire where animals are closely congregated. Once contracted, your dog is likely to cough persistently for three weeks or so but usually is not lethargic or particularly off-colour. Exceptions are puppies and also very elderly dogs which are at much greater risk.

Recent work has shown that there are very virulent causal agents that can cause a serious disease with the onset of rapid broncho-pneumonia, followed by death if aggressive treatment is not rapidly instituted.

A vaccine is available in the form of nasal drops. It is extremely effective and will give a workable immunity within five days of administration. However, like the immune response to the natural disease, protection is relatively short-lived. Therefore, dogs that are exposed to special risks should be revaccinated every six to ten months to maintain immunity.

Recently, an intranasal vaccine (nasal drops), incorporating not only the Bordetella organisms but also parainfluenza virus, has become available. This vaccine is another step in the control of this undoubtedly unpleasant condition, but, as with human winter coughs and sneezes, we are still some way from total eradication.

Canine Coronavirus

Canine coronavirus enteritis can cause diarrhoea, particularly in puppies. The disease is usually mild and responds well to supportive therapy, although the virus may be shed in the faeces for two to three weeks after recovery. A vaccine is available in North America and some parts of Europe, but there is no licensed vaccine currently available in Britain.

Lyme Disease (Borreliosis)

This bacterial disease is carried by certain ticks whose bite can transmit the disease to dogs and people. It is very common in parts of North America and does occur in the UK. It causes acute polyarthritis in both dogs and people, and sometimes fever, heart, kidney, and neurological problems can also occur.

PARASITE CONTROL

Parasite control is important with all dogs, irrespective of their lifestyle. Parasites are roughly divided into two groups

- Ectoparasites (which live on the surface of the host – e.g. fleas, lice, ticks and mites)
- Endoparasites (which live inside the host – such as worms).

The Flea

Fleas are the most common ectoparasites on dogs. They are found worldwide and are no strangers to the Dachshund. They can be the initiators of other skin problems in this breed. Some dogs will carry very high flea burdens with apparent unconcern, whereas others will show signs of flea allergy dermatitis although no evidence of fleas can be found. This is due to the development of a hypersensitivity to flea saliva. Fortunately not particularly common in the Dachshund, it can be the cause of serious itching with large areas of hair loss. Careful diagnosis is then necessary, since Dachshunds are susceptible to other conditions that can cause hair loss (such as hyperthyroidism – see page 127, Cushing's disease – see page 125 and mange – see page 115).

Although the adult flea lays eggs on the dog, these soon drop to the ground. Provided temperature and humidity are within the correct range, they soon develop into larvae (immature forms) in your carpets or in the gaps between

The dog flea – Ctenocephalides.

the floorboards. Development can also take place outside, provided the temperature and humidity are fairly high. Adult fleas must have a meal of blood to complete their life cycle and commence egg-laying.

Flea Treatment

There are many effective preparations to control adult fleas on the animal. Sprays and prolonged-action spot-on preparations are probably the most effective.

Adult fleas account for only approximately five per cent of the total flea population. Control of the 95 per cent of immature stages can be much more difficult. Few environmental insecticides have any effect against flea larvae, so an insecticide with prolonged action should be used that will be effective against subsequently emerging adults.

In addition, control can involve oral medication given to your dog, which will prevent the completion of the life cycle of the flea. The compound is transferred to the adult flea when it bites the dog for the all-essential blood meal. The compound, which is harmless to the dog, prevents larval development.

Flea control not only involves the eradication of adult fleas from the dog; environmental control is also needed. Thorough vacuuming to remove immature stages is recommended. Obviously, it is difficult to control developing fleas in the garden (yard), particularly if outdoor-living Dachshunds are continuously reinfested by visiting wildlife (such as rats, racoons, hedgehogs, or cats).

Lice

Lice are not as common as fleas. Unlike fleas, the whole life cycle occurs on the dog, and the eggs (nits) are sticky and attach to individual hairs. Lice invariably cause intense itching and are not uncommon on dogs that spend most of their time outside. Since they do not infest the environment, close contact between dogs is necessary to spread the parasites, therefore they are not uncommon in dogs acquired from puppy farms/mills.

Heavy infestation can cause anaemia, in addition to sometimes quite serious skin lesions caused by self-mutilation (due to the irritation).

Eradication is relatively simple since most flea preparations are effective, as is bathing in insecticidal shampoo.

However, it must be remembered that most insecticidal shampoos do not have residual action and therefore reinfestation (i.e. contact with potentially louse-infested dogs) must be prevented.

Ticks

Ticks are carriers of various diseases, such as Lyme disease (which has already been mentioned (see page 110); Babesiosis and Ehrlichiosis are other examples.

At present, these diseases are not recognised as a problem in the UK, although they are major problems in warmer parts of Europe and the United States.

Several flea and lice preparations are also licensed for tick control – your vet will advise you on the best choice.

Harvest Mites

These are the larvae of a mite that lives in decaying organic matter. Red in colour, the mites are just visible to the naked eye and are picked up by dogs exercised in fields and woodlands, particularly with chalky soils. The feet and muzzle are most commonly affected and the mites can cause intense irritation.

Again, the use of prolonged-action preparations is recommended.

Cheyletiellosis

Cheyletiella yasguri, the causal mite, can just be seen by the naked eye as white specks, hence the term 'walking dandruff'. The condition is not uncommon in puppies acquired from large kennels or from puppy farms/mills. The mite is zoonotic and causes intense irritation, particularly in children. Symptomless adult dogs (carriers) are usually the source of infection in kennels.

Mange

Mange is a parasitic skin disease caused by microscopic mites. Two types cause problems in dogs: demodectic and sarcoptic mites.

The former is caused by demodex mites, which are present in the hair follicles and sebaceous glands of many dogs. Sometimes, for unexplained reasons, the mites will start to multiply and cause inflammation and hair loss. This is not uncommon in the Dachshund, which tends to be over-represented in this respect. Demodectic mange is frequently seen in poorly-reared puppies when secondary infection will make the condition a great deal worse.

Puppies will often acquire the demodectic mites in small numbers from their mother while suckling. It is only if there is a triggering mechanism that lowers the pup's innate immunity that development of signs of the disease will occur. Therefore, demodectic mange is not considered a contagious disease, unlike sarcoptic mange.

Modern treatments are effective, but it is important that you consult your vet with any concerns regarding the skin of your Dachshund since there may be other, underlying causes of the condition.

'Puppies often acquire mange mites when suckling'

Sarcoptic mange is zoonotic and is known as scabies when it occurs in humans. Children are particularly susceptible, often developing intensely itching lesions on their arms and abdomen as a result of contact with the mangy dog.

Modern treatment for sarcoptic mange not only includes baths and lotions, but also drugs taken internally.

Roundworms

These are the most common endoparasites in the dog. *Toxocara canis*, the most common, is a large roundworm, 7-15 cms (3-6 ins) long. The life cycle in the dog is complicated and larvae (immature forms) can remain dormant in various tissues within your Dachshund for long periods. In the female, under the influence of the hormones of pregnancy, these immature forms become reactivated. They cross the

All puppies carry a burden of roundworms, so worming is essential.

placental barrier and finally develop into adult worms in the small intestine of the puppy.

Humans, particularly children, can occasionally become infected, so regular worming of your Dachshund is a wise precaution. Effective remedies are available without prescription from pet outlets, but it is worthwhile consulting your veterinary surgeon in order to formulate a comprehensive deworming strategy, particularly if you have young children.

Often, infestation goes unnoticed, but, if there is a heavy worm burden, the puppy will grow poorly and have recurrent diarrhoea and vomiting. Sometimes live worms are passed, and, occasionally, obstruction of the bowel – and death – can occur.

In puppies, a regular worming programme should be undertaken. This often commences as early as two weeks of age. The regular programme should be continued into adulthood. Your vet will advise you.

Tapeworms

Tapeworms or cestodes are the other major class of worms found in the dog. Unlike roundworms, they have an indirect life cycle so that spread is not directly from dog to dog but must involve an intermediate host that varies according to the type of tapeworm.

Dipylidium caninum is the most common tapeworm of the dog and uses the flea as the intermediate host. These worms, measuring up to 50 cms (20 ins), live in the intestine. Eggs are contained within the mature segments, which look like grains of rice and are shed from the end of the worm and passed out in the dog's faeces.

Flea larvae ingest the microscopic eggs, which mature as the flea develops. The mature flea is then swallowed by the dog and so the life cycle of the tapeworm is completed.

Effective tapeworm remedies, like those for roundworms, are widely available without prescription. However, effective eradication involves rigorous control of the flea, including the developing larvae in the environment. It is, therefore, worthwhile discussing the problem with your vet at the outset.

Dachshunds are great hunters, and, if they regularly catch and eat rabbits, hares, and similar wildlife, they can infect themselves with the *Taenia* species of tapeworm for which such prey act as intermediate hosts.

Tapeworm infections are uncommon in puppies. Usually the first signs noted are the little wriggling 'rice grains' around the dog's anus. These are the mature segments packed with eggs that have to be eaten by the appropriate intermediate host to complete the life cycle.

Echinococcus species of tapeworm are also of importance in the dog, because of their zoonotic potential. In Britain, there are local areas of infection, particularly in Wales. With the recent relaxation of quarantine regulations, any dogs entering Britain from Europe have to be specially treated with specific remedies against *Echinococcus multilocularis*, which can cause serious cysts in the lungs in people. In North America, the problem is also localised, affecting mainly rural areas of the south-west with large sheep populations.

There are effective tapeworm remedies covering all species. Your veterinarian will prescribe and advise.

Heartworm

This worm, *Dirofilaria immitis*, causes major

'Being a great hunter, the Dachshund is prone to tapeworms'

problems in many of the warmer parts of the world, including parts of North America. Effective drugs are available. Consult your vet if heartworm is a problem in your location.

Other Worms

Hookworms (*Uncinaria* and *Anclostoma* species) together with whipworms (*Trichuris vulpis*) are occasionally the cause of lack of condition, with sometimes more severe signs such as anaemia and dysentery. They are more common in Dachshunds in North America and other parts of the world than in the UK. These worms are usually discovered in puppies and occasionally adult dogs during routine faecal investigations.

Treatment with modern dewormers prescribed by your vet will effectively clear the problems.

Giardia And Coccidia

Microscopic endoparasites, such as the protozoan parasites of the Giardia and Coccidia species, can cause diarrhoea problems, particularly in puppies.

Giardia, a water-borne disease, is more common in North America than in Britain, although it can be a problem in the UK in imported dogs (and may increase with the relaxation of quarantine regulations).

Giardiasis is considered to be zoonotic – and is the most common intestinal parasite in humans in America. Nevertheless, there is no conclusive evidence that cysts shed by dogs and cats are infective for humans.

EMERGENCY CARE AND FIRST AID

Emergencies do not simply involve road traffic accidents – bites, burns, heat stroke, insect stings and poisoning can all happen accidentally and unexpectedly.

First aid is the initial treatment given in an emergency. The purpose is to preserve life, to reduce pain and discomfort, and to minimise the risk of permanent disability and disfigurement. Irrespective of the emergency, there is much that can be done by simple first aid.

Priorities

1. Keep calm and do not panic.
2. Get help. Contact your veterinary surgeon, explain the situation and obtain first aid advice specific for the situation.
3. If there is the possibility of internal injury, try to keep your dog as still as possible, placing him in a box or other makeshift container in order to restrain him.
4. If your Dachshund is in shock, try to keep your Dachshund as warm as possible. Blankets are ideal, if available; otherwise, wrap him in a coat or even cover him with newspaper.
5. Move the injured dog in the container, if possible. However, if not totally enclosed, make sure he is sufficiently restrained so that he does not try to jump out in panic.
6. Take him to the vet as soon as you can, if possible getting someone to travel in the car with you to help. If you cannot get help, make sure the container is wedged so that the dog does not move in case of a sudden

The responsible owner should be well-versed in first aid procedures.

stop and also so that he cannot get out and injure himself further.

7. Drive carefully and observe the speed limits.

Essential Principles

The ABC of first aid is paramount in any emergency situation.

- **A (Airway)**
  Ensure that there is no obstruction preventing air (oxygen) from reaching the lungs
- **B (Breathing)**
  Make sure the dog is breathing
- **C (Circulation)**
  Make sure the heart is beating.

These principles are vital. Do not, however, take risks. If your dog is having difficulty breathing, be very careful if you place your fingers in the mouth – he could well bite in fright. Use a tie, a piece of string or twine, or even a pair of tights, to pry the jaws apart. Sometimes a piece of bone or stick can be seen stuck across the back of the mouth and may be dislodged with an implement such as the handle of a spoon or your hand protected with a thick glove.

If your dog is not breathing, try gently pumping the chest with your hand, at the same time feeling just behind the elbow for a heart beat (pulse). If none is detected, start cardiac massage. In a Miniature Dachshund, this can be carried out with one hand by gently squeezing the rib cage just behind the elbows with the fingers and thumb of one hand. With a Standard Dachshund, both hands should be used, one on either side of the chest. Squeeze gently approximately 20-25 times a minute. This has the dual function of stimulating the heart, and, at the same time, helps to get air into the lungs. Stop every 10 squeezes or so to see if you can detect a heart beat or any breathing.

Shock

Shock is a complex condition, disrupting the delicate fluid balance in the body. It always results in a serious fall in blood pressure. This can be due to severe bleeding, heart failure and other causes.

Signs include rapid breathing and an increase in heart rate. The mucous membranes of the gums, lips and under the eyelids look pale and the dog may appear depressed. His feet or ears may feel cold to the touch, and vomiting can occur.

- Give first aid treatment for shock
- Keep your Dachshund warm
- Keep him as quiet as possible
- Seek immediate veterinary help, particularly if haemorrhaging is present. If you are unable to bandage the bleeding area, try to control this using finger or hand pressure.

Bleeding

Cut pads and torn nails, in particular, are not uncommon in Dachshunds. They can be extremely painful and bleed profusely. Try to bandage the cut tightly, using any clean material if a bandage is not readily available.

A polythene bag placed over the paw, between the layers of bandage, will contain the blood. Try to ensure that blood loss is kept to a minimum and get your pet to the vet without delay. Do not leave a tight bandage in place for more than 15-20 minutes. If necessary, partially unwrap the bandage and then re-apply.

If bleeding is from a site that cannot be bandaged, try to control it by applying finger or hand pressure with a piece of clean dressing (such as a handkerchief), between your hand and the wound.

Burns And Scalds

Cool the burned area with cold water as quickly as possible. If necessary, place your dog in the bath or sink, then, applying a cold wet dressing (such as a clean, wet towel), take him to your vet as soon as possible, keeping the area moist.

Caustic materials (such as drain and oven cleaners) can burn, so try to dilute with plenty of cold water. If the dog has licked the material, use cloths soaked in clean cold water, and press them between the jaws.

Eye Injuries

The most common eye injuries are caused by grass seeds, or scratches from bushes and cats' claws. Cold water, or better still saline solution (contact lens solution), liberally applied with a pad, should be used to cleanse the eye. Then seek veterinary help as soon as possible.

Heat Stroke

Heat stroke can strike any breed, particularly if left in a car. Remember, the car need not necessarily be in direct sunlight to kill your dog.

First signs are excessive panting with obvious distress. Coma and death can quickly follow. Reduce the temperature by bathing your Dachshund in cool water. Place ice on the gums, under the tail, and in the groin area. Cover the still-wet animal in damp towels and take him to the vet as soon as possible. If driving, keep the windows open during the journey, as evaporation will help to reduce his body temperature.

Fits And Seizures

While the dog is in the fit or seizure, it is better not to touch him unnecessarily. If he can be confined in a large cardboard carton or similar container, he is less likely to frighten himself when coming out of the fit.

Try to keep him in as dim a light as possible and remember that, once recovered, he will be dazed and unable to see or hear properly at first. Exercise caution since, for a short time, he may not be able to recognise you and may bite you.

If the fit lasts more than three to four minutes, contact your vet for instructions; otherwise, once he appears recovered, take him to the practice for a check-up.

BREED-ASSOCIATED CONDITIONS

The most commonly quoted conditions associated with the breed involve the eye and the spine, although skin, hormonal and urinary problems are also linked with the Dachshund.

EYE CONDITIONS

Distichiasis

This condition is caused by the presence of a double row of eyelashes, which can impinge upon the eyeball. This leads to conjunctivitis and spasm of the muscles of the eyelid so that the eye is kept tightly closed. It can cause severe damage to the cornea, and, if untreated, can result in blindness.

Treatment, where the offending lashes are surgically removed, is very successful. If you notice your Dachshund has excessively wet eyes, due to tear overflow, is repeatedly rubbing at the eyes with the paw, or there is any discharge or soreness, consult your veterinary surgeon without delay.

Genetic factors may be involved, particularly when one considers that, in the make-up of the modern Dachshund, spaniel breeds and Pinschers (all affected by distichiasis) are reputed to have played a part.

Entropion

This involves the inversion or inward turning of the eyelids, usually the lower lid. As the hair-covered eyelid rolls inward, the hairs impinge upon the sensitive eyeball, hence the effect is similar to distichiasis with excessive watering (tearing) and discomfort, causing the dog to paw at the eye, either pawing at it or rubbing it along the ground. This irritation inflames the lids which swell and turn inwards even more – so the condition perpetuates itself.

Causes can be genetic (primary entropion), but in the Dachshund many cases are due to injury or irritation (secondary entropion). Even Miniature Dachshunds are basically hunters. They love to chase through undergrowth and can injure the eyelids in this way.

All breeding stock must be eye-tested.

If your Dachshund suddenly has a tightly-closed eye, try to part the lids gently to examine for any visible damage or foreign body – such as a grass seed lodged beneath the lid.

With all eye problems, consult your vet without delay. Even tiny eyelid wounds which do not appear to concern the dog may heal and cause scarring, which, in turn, can lead to entropion and other problems.

Ectropion

Ectropion is the opposite of entropion – the lid turns outwards and the eyelid appears to droop. In the Dachshund, this is mainly an acquired condition following injury. Successful surgical techniques are available.

Progressive Retinal Atrophy (PRA)

This gradually impairs the dog's vision and can result in blindness. Generalised PRA is recognised, particularly in Miniature Dachshunds (especially the Long-haired Dachshund and Smooth varieties). The problems of PRA are minimal in the Dachshund, compared with some other breeds.

It is an inherited condition for which there is no treatment. Eradication schemes are available on both sides of the Atlantic.

Optic Nerve Hypoplasia

This condition, which is basically lack of proper development of the optic nerve, is another possible genetic condition and occurs in the Miniature Long-haired variety. Affected dogs are visually impaired and there is no treatment.

Persistant Pupillary Membrane (PMM)

This is another possible hereditary problem at present under investigation in Miniature Wire-haired Dachshunds. It can result in corneal opacities (i.e. cloudiness of the clear part of the front of the eye) or actual cataracts (cloudiness or opacity of the lens within the eye). Although the lesions may be present from birth, they are often not noticed until later in life, unless careful specialist ophthalmological examination has been carried out for some other reason.

The condition is known to be hereditary in Basenjis and other breeds. Occasionally, cataract surgery may be required.

Keratoconjunctivitis Sicca (KCS)

Seen classically in West Highland White Terriers, the condition also occurs in Dachshunds. This condition, also known as 'dry eye', causes a very chronic conjunctivitis with considerable inflammation of the conjunctiva and also thickening and drying of the cornea. Because the eye itches, not surprisingly the dog cannot resist rubbing the eye, thus exacerbating the condition.

The problem can be managed medically with tear substitutes and also special drops which often have to be applied long-term. Surgery is recommended if the loss of tear production is absolute and permanent. It involves the transposition of the duct of one of the salivary glands into the eye (saliva and tears are biochemically very similar). The operation, routinely performed by veterinary ophthalmologists, carries a high rate of success.

Wall Eye

Also known as heterochromia iridis, this condition is seen particularly in dappled Dachshunds. The eyes may have different coloured irises or only part of one iris may be a different colour. There is no loss of vision and the Breed Standard allows wall eyes in dapples.

Microphthalmia

This may be inherited and indicates that one or both eyes are abnormally small. Usually, the affected eye is sightless, but the condition is not painful. It may be an inherited defect.

SKELETAL PROBLEMS

The fact that Dachshunds can suffer back problems is well known.

The British Breed Standard states: "the length of the back and the character of the discs between the vertebrae of the spine have a tendency to allow a weakening in the area and it is therefore important that the loin should be short and strong, and that individuals should not be allowed to become obese."

Despite the association of Dachshunds and backs, there is no established genetic basis for this weakness. Like the Bulldog and the Basset, the Dachshund is a chondrodystrophoid. Chondrodystrophy is a disorder in cartilage formation. It can be associated with degeneration of intervertebral discs.

Intervertebral discs are essentially 'shock absorbers' between the bones of the spine (vertebrae). They appear to be subject to damage much earlier in the Dachshund and this causes pressure on the delicate spinal cord. The most common sites are in the neck or at the junction between the ribs and the loin.

Symptoms

Signs can vary from mild neck pain to paralysis involving all four limbs, depending on the severity.

Initially, slight stiffness and some limb weakness (paresis) are the only signs. Dogs of three to five years of age are most commonly affected. This will often follow fairly strenuous exercise, leading owners to think the dog has just overdone it a little, since frequently, after rest, all appears to be well. However, recurrence can result in rapid escalation from stiffness or paresis, to total paralysis.

If you see one or more episodes of stiffness in your relatively young Dachshund, discuss the matter with your veterinarian.

Modern veterinary treatment for intervertebral disc disease now carries a far better prognosis than even just a few years ago.

However, early diagnosis and treatment is imperative if paralysis is to be reversed. In most cases, not only will your pet be unable to walk but will also be unable to perform natural functions.

Therefore it is essential that supportive nursing is instituted without delay, so that secondary problems (due to the inability to pass urine, for example) are avoided.

Treatment for intervertebral disc disease often involves surgery to relieve pressure, and carries a good prognosis.

Treatment for spinal problems is improving, but it can be expensive.

Diagnosis

Diagnosis may involve more than plain X-rays (radiography). Techniques may include myelography, when a special dye is introduced into the vertebral canal to pinpoint the area of pressure caused by the ruptured or slipped disc. You may be referred to a specialist, and this can be expensive as can subsequent treatment, which may involve complicated spinal surgery. Pet health insurance, taken out as soon as possible after acquiring your Dachshund, is a wise decision. Be sure to check what conditions are covered by your policy.

Treatment

Sometimes surgery is not necessary and other forms of treatment, involving sophisticated anti-inflammatories and pain-killers, may be prescribed. Whatever the treatment, as soon as your dog is recovering, restriction of exercise is very important. Dachshunds are energetic, active dogs, and, as soon as they feel better, they want to continue enjoying life to the full. Therefore, your vet may advise hospitalisation for what may, to you, seem a protracted period; alternatively cage/crate rest at home, sometimes for several weeks, may be advised.

With the exception of disc problems, Dachshunds suffer little from the bone and joint diseases which beset many other pedigree dogs. No doubt this is a reflection of their healthy, active working ancestry. Thus, knee problems, so common in many active dogs, are virtually unknown in Dachshunds, as is hip dysplasia and other hip-related conditions.

SKIN PROBLEMS

Acanthosis Nigrans

This is a fairly common condition in Dachshunds. A hormonal basis has been put forward, but most cases are described as idiopathic (i.e. occurring without known cause). The signs are thickening and blackening of the skin, especially in the armpits. Sometimes, it affects other joints where there is close contact between the skin surfaces. Secondary infection will often lead to irritation (pruritis). Treatment can be lifelong and involve special shampoos and sometimes chemotherapy. Usually the lesions are symmetrical.

Alopecia (Hair Loss)

This also occurs in the breed, especially affecting the ears of adult dogs. Sometimes it can be due to low-grade mange infestation (see page 115) and will respond with appropriate treatment. Other cases may be inherited and may be colour-associated, since alopecia is known to occur in association with the gene for colour dilution, in which case there is no treatment.

Pemphigus Foliaceus

This is an auto-immune disease, characterised by generalised scaling, frequently resulting in loss of hair on the nose and ears. It has been suggested that Dachshunds may be more prone to this condition than other breeds. It is also possible that some of the alopecia conditions in the breed may be due to this cause.

URINARY DISORDERS

Cystinuria

Cystine is an amino acid, which is filtered by the renal tubules and is reabsorbed while passing through the kidney. However, in dogs predisposed to cystine stones (uroliths), only 80 to 90 per cent is reabsorbed, the other 10 to 20 per cent appearing in the urine. The problem appears to affect only males, and is a sex-linked recessive trait.

Signs will occur suddenly. An energetic, healthy and happy dog will suddenly appear to have great difficulty passing urine. This is a serious situation and your vet should be consulted without delay.

Treatment may involve surgery to relieve the immediate blockage, plus medication to control the condition.

Although cystine comprises approximately only 1 per cent of all uroliths found in dogs, Dachshunds contribute to a significant number of these cases. Following treatment, symptoms can recur and sometimes other bladder stones – which can affect dogs of any age or sex – will be involved.

HORMONE PROBLEMS

In comparison with other breeds, Dachshunds appear to be particularly prone to three hormonal conditions, detailed below.

Cushing's Disease

Also known as hyperadrenocorticism, Cushing's disease is associated with the production of excessive levels of cortisol (cortisone) from the adrenal glands. This can be due to:

- The adrenal gland producing too much cortisone, usually due to an adrenal gland tumour. In dogs, this is a rare condition but Dachshunds do tend to be more prone to adrenal adenomas (tumours) than other dogs.
- A tumour of the pituitary gland in the brain. This is the most common cause of Cushing's disease, amounting to 85 per cent of all cases. The tumour stimulates the gland to overproduce certain hormones, which have a direct effect on the adrenal glands producing excessive amounts of cortisol.

Whether the tumour is within the adrenal gland or the pituitary gland, it may be either benign or malignant.

The clinical signs of Cushing's disease are sometimes vague and non-specific. There is an increase in appetite, water consumption and urination. Lethargy, poor appetite and a bloated abdomen soon follow. Since middle-aged Dachshunds frequently run to fat, these early signs are often overlooked until it is time for the annual booster. Then your vet may have suspicions and suggest carrying out certain blood tests which reveal the true cause of the sudden ageing and apparent obese appearance of your dog.

Other signs include a lack of hair growth, particularly on the flanks. The hair often lacks

Dachshunds can be prone to hormonal conditions.

pigment and appears greyish in colour. The skin may also look paper-thin.

Cushing's disease usually occurs in middle-aged to older dogs but Dachshunds are notable in that quite young dogs can be affected with the condition.

Blood tests can predict the site of the tumour. If a benign adrenal-based tumour is responsible, surgical removal will result in a cure. Otherwise, sophisticated medical treatment is available that will control the condition and allow the dog to lead a normal life on a long-term basis.

Diabetes

Diabetes is a general term covering conditions that result in increased thirst and increased urination. There are two forms in dogs: diabetes insipidus and diabetes mellitus.

Diabetes insipidus is a relatively rare condition and indicates the body's inability to control water balance. Diabetes mellitus is sugar diabetes, which occurs if the dog is either unable to produce adequate amounts of insulin, or if the dog cannot utilise any insulin that is produced.

Diabetes is usually a disease of middle or old age in dogs, but in the Dachshund it can occur in young adults. Unspayed females are more prone than males, mainly due to hormones associated with the oestrous cycle.

The four classic signs of diabetes are:
• Weight loss
• Increased appetite
• Increased water consumption
• Increased urination.

Watch for increased thirst or increased appetite, as both can be early signs of diabetes.

These symptoms will alert the owner to something amiss. Your vet will confirm the diagnosis by urine and blood tests.

The condition is not curable, but it can be controlled in dogs once you have mastered the technique of urine testing and daily insulin administration, both of which are quite simple and will be carefully demonstrated and supervised initially by your vet.

Consistency is the vital component of proper management of the diabetic dog. There has to be consistent feeding, a stable, stress-free lifestyle, and regular medication. If your diabetic pet happens to be an entire female Dachshund, do not be alarmed if your vet suggests ovariohysterectomy (neutering) since this will make long-term stabilisation very much easier for you.

Untreated diabetes leads to serious and often irreversible liver changes. It is important that, if you have any suspicions, you consult your vet without delay, taking a urine sample with you if possible.

Hypothyroidism

The Dachshund is one of a number of breeds that has a predisposition to hypothyroidism, a decreased production of thyroid hormones. These, produced by the thyroid gland located in the neck near the trachea (windpipe), regulate metabolism (body chemistry). When they are lacking, the metabolism slows down and the clinical signs of hypothyroidism become apparent.

Virtually every organ in the body is affected, so there are plenty of signs – weight gain without an increase in appetite, lethargy, and general lack of desire to exercise even in relatively young dogs. Skin signs include a dry hair coat with excessive shedding, resulting in general thinness of hair. It is often noted that the hair fails to regrow if it is clipped. The skin appears darker due to increased pigmentation of the skin. Unneutered animals tend to become infertile and oestrus often ceases in bitches.

Like diabetes, hypothyroidism is treatable but not curable. Treatment involves the daily administration of tablets once diagnosis has been confirmed by your veterinary surgeon. Blood tests have to be repeated periodically during the course of treatment to ensure the thyroid hormone blood levels are within the correct range.

GASTRIC DILATION/VOLVULUS

This condition occurs most frequently in large, deep-chested dogs, such as Great Danes, German Shepherd Dogs, Irish Setters, and others. It is occasionally seen in smaller breeds, including the Dachshund.

Commonly called bloat, it involves the dog's stomach distending with gas to the point that the pressure affects other vital organs and death can follow very quickly.

If your Dachshund appears to be at all uncomfortable, especially after a large meal, check the abdomen. If it appears to be swelling, particularly on the left side, behind the rib cage, it is imperative to call your vet without delay.

CANCER

Dachshunds are not specifically prone to tumours, with the exception of malignant melanomas involving the mouth and oral mucous membranes. These often start as dark-coloured growths on the gums or palate. If you notice anything unusual in your Dachshund's mouth, contact your vet.

DENTAL PROBLEMS

Dachshunds, like many of the smaller breeds, are prone to periodontitis, an inflammation of the gums and associated tissues. Miniature Dachshunds are more prone than Standards but today, with modern dental home-care remedies and special diets, the common sight of the toothless, 10-year-old Miniature Dachshund of yesteryear is hopefully a thing of the past!

To prevent early tooth loss, regular dental home care is essential. It is worthwhile discussing this aspect with your vet at the time of primary vaccination. In this way, the puppy can be trained to accept regular mouth inspections and cleaning.

With good care and management, your Dachshund should live a long and healthy life.

CRYPTORCHIDISM

Cryptorchid means 'hidden testes'. The testes of the dog are contained within the abdomen at birth, but normally descend into the scrotum within 7-10 days. A cryptorchid is an animal with one or both testes retained somewhere along the normal path of testicular descent. A definite diagnosis cannot be made as to whether one or both testes is/are permanently absent from the scrotum until the dog reaches puberty.

If, by the time your Dachshund is 6-9 months old, both testes are not where they should be, contact your veterinarian. Retained testes carry an increased risk of becoming cancerous and there is also the risk of torsion (twisting) of the spermatic cord and blood vessels.

The condition appears to be inherited. The Miniature Dachshund appears to have a particular predisposition to the condition. Both the male and the female may carry the gene responsible. Therefore, ideally, neither parent, in addition to the cryptorchid animal, should be bred. Bilateral cryptorchid dogs are willing and able to mate, although seldom fertile. Unilateral cryptorchids can sire litters and are thus able to pass the problem on to future generations.

FINAL NOTE

Despite the problems listed, the Dachshund is generally a healthy, robust little soul, who is an asset to any home. This miniature hound with his bold, affectionate and clownish ways, is simply a joy to share your life and your home with.